Secrets of the

NCSF-CPT Exam

SECRETS

Study Guide
Your Key to Exam Success

NCSF Test Review for the National Council on Strength and Fitness Personal Trainer Exam

Dear Future Exam Success Story:

First of all, **THANK YOU** for purchasing Mometrix study materials!

Second, congratulations! You are one of the few determined test-takers who are committed to doing whatever it takes to excel on your exam. **You have come to the right place.** We developed these study materials with one goal in mind: to deliver you the information you need in a format that's concise and easy to use.

In addition to optimizing your guide for the content of the test, we've outlined our recommended steps for breaking down the preparation process into small, attainable goals so you can make sure you stay on track.

We've also analyzed the entire test-taking process, identifying the most common pitfalls and showing how you can overcome them and be ready for any curveball the test throws you.

Standardized testing is one of the biggest obstacles on your road to success, which only increases the importance of doing well in the high-pressure, high-stakes environment of test day. Your results on this test could have a significant impact on your future, and this guide provides the information and practical advice to help you achieve your full potential on test day.

Your success is our success

We would love to hear from you! If you would like to share the story of your exam success or if you have any questions or comments in regard to our products, please contact us at **800-673-8175** or **support@mometrix.com**.

Thanks again for your business and we wish you continued success!

Sincerely,
The Mometrix Test Preparation Team

Need more help? Check out our flashcards at: http://mometrixflashcards.com/NCSF

Written and edited by the Mometrix Exam Secrets Test Prep Team
Printed in the United States of America

TABLE OF CONTENTS

Introduction

Thank you for purchasing this resource! You have made the choice to prepare yourself for a test that could have a huge impact on your future, and this guide is designed to help you be fully ready for test day. Obviously, it's important to have a solid understanding of the test material, but you also need to be prepared for the unique environment and stressors of the test, so that you can perform to the best of your abilities.

For this purpose, the first section that appears in this guide is the **Secret Keys**. We've devoted countless hours to meticulously researching what works and what doesn't, and we've boiled down our findings to the five most impactful steps you can take to improve your performance on the test. We start at the beginning with study planning and move through the preparation process, all the way to the testing strategies that will help you get the most out of what you know when you're finally sitting in front of the test.

We recommend that you start preparing for your test as far in advance as possible. However, if you've bought this guide as a last-minute study resource and only have a few days before your test, we recommend that you skip over the first two Secret Keys since they address a long-term study plan.

If you struggle with **test anxiety**, we strongly encourage you to check out our recommendations for how you can overcome it. Test anxiety is a formidable foe, but it can be beaten, and we want to make sure you have the tools you need to defeat it.

Secret Key #1 – Plan Big, Study Small

There's a lot riding on your performance. If you want to ace this test, you're going to need to keep your skills sharp and the material fresh in your mind. You need a plan that lets you review everything you need to know while still fitting in your schedule. We'll break this strategy down into three categories.

Information Organization

Start with the information you already have: the official test outline. From this, you can make a complete list of all the concepts you need to cover before the test. Organize these concepts into groups that can be studied together, and create a list of any related vocabulary you need to learn so you can brush up on any difficult terms. You'll want to keep this vocabulary list handy once you actually start studying since you may need to add to it along the way.

Time Management

Once you have your set of study concepts, decide how to spread them out over the time you have left before the test. Break your study plan into small, clear goals so you have a manageable task for each day and know exactly what you're doing. Then just focus on one small step at a time. When you manage your time this way, you don't need to spend hours at a time studying. Studying a small block of content for a short period each day helps you retain information better and avoid stressing over how much you have left to do. You can relax knowing that you have a plan to cover everything in time. In order for this strategy to be effective though, you have to start studying early and stick to your schedule. Avoid the exhaustion and futility that comes from last-minute cramming!

Study Environment

The environment you study in has a big impact on your learning. Studying in a coffee shop, while probably more enjoyable, is not likely to be as fruitful as studying in a quiet room. It's important to keep distractions to a minimum. You're only planning to study for a short block of time, so make the most of it. Don't pause to check your phone or get up to find a snack. It's also important to **avoid multitasking**. Research has consistently shown that multitasking will make your studying dramatically less effective. Your study area should also be comfortable and well-lit so you don't have the distraction of straining your eyes or sitting on an uncomfortable chair.

The time of day you study is also important. You want to be rested and alert. Don't wait until just before bedtime. Study when you'll be most likely to comprehend and remember. Even better, if you know what time of day your test will be, set that time aside for study. That way your brain will be used to working on that subject at that specific time and you'll have a better chance of recalling information.

Finally, it can be helpful to team up with others who are studying for the same test. Your actual studying should be done in as isolated an environment as possible, but the work of organizing the information and setting up the study plan can be divided up. In between study sessions, you can discuss with your teammates the concepts that you're all studying and quiz each other on the details. Just be sure that your teammates are as serious about the test as you are. If you find that your study time is being replaced with social time, you might need to find a new team.

Secret Key #2 – Make Your Studying Count

You're devoting a lot of time and effort to preparing for this test, so you want to be absolutely certain it will pay off. This means doing more than just reading the content and hoping you can remember it on test day. It's important to make every minute of study count. There are two main areas you can focus on to make your studying count:

Retention

It doesn't matter how much time you study if you can't remember the material. You need to make sure you are retaining the concepts. To check your retention of the information you're learning, try recalling it at later times with minimal prompting. Try carrying around flashcards and glance at one or two from time to time or ask a friend who's also studying for the test to quiz you.

To enhance your retention, look for ways to put the information into practice so that you can apply it rather than simply recalling it. If you're using the information in practical ways, it will be much easier to remember. Similarly, it helps to solidify a concept in your mind if you're not only reading it to yourself but also explaining it to someone else. Ask a friend to let you teach them about a concept you're a little shaky on (or speak aloud to an imaginary audience if necessary). As you try to summarize, define, give examples, and answer your friend's questions, you'll understand the concepts better and they will stay with you longer. Finally, step back for a big picture view and ask yourself how each piece of information fits with the whole subject. When you link the different concepts together and see them working together as a whole, it's easier to remember the individual components.

Finally, practice showing your work on any multi-step problems, even if you're just studying. Writing out each step you take to solve a problem will help solidify the process in your mind, and you'll be more likely to remember it during the test.

Modality

Modality simply refers to the means or method by which you study. Choosing a study modality that fits your own individual learning style is crucial. No two people learn best in exactly the same way, so it's important to know your strengths and use them to your advantage.

For example, if you learn best by visualization, focus on visualizing a concept in your mind and draw an image or a diagram. Try color-coding your notes, illustrating them, or creating symbols that will trigger your mind to recall a learned concept. If you learn best by hearing or discussing information, find a study partner who learns the same way or read aloud to yourself. Think about how to put the information in your own words. Imagine that you are giving a lecture on the topic and record yourself so you can listen to it later.

For any learning style, flashcards can be helpful. Organize the information so you can take advantage of spare moments to review. Underline key words or phrases. Use different colors for different categories. Mnemonic devices (such as creating a short list in which every item starts with the same letter) can also help with retention. Find what works best for you and use it to store the information in your mind most effectively and easily.

Secret Key #3 – Practice the Right Way

Your success on test day depends not only on how many hours you put into preparing, but also on whether you prepared the right way. It's good to check along the way to see if your studying is paying off. One of the most effective ways to do this is by taking practice tests to evaluate your progress. Practice tests are useful because they show exactly where you need to improve. Every time you take a practice test, pay special attention to these three groups of questions:

- The questions you got wrong
- The questions you had to guess on, even if you guessed right
- The questions you found difficult or slow to work through

This will show you exactly what your weak areas are, and where you need to devote more study time. Ask yourself why each of these questions gave you trouble. Was it because you didn't understand the material? Was it because you didn't remember the vocabulary? Do you need more repetitions on this type of question to build speed and confidence? Dig into those questions and figure out how you can strengthen your weak areas as you go back to review the material.

Additionally, many practice tests have a section explaining the answer choices. It can be tempting to read the explanation and think that you now have a good understanding of the concept. However, an explanation likely only covers part of the question's broader context. Even if the explanation makes sense, **go back and investigate** every concept related to the question until you're positive you have a thorough understanding.

As you go along, keep in mind that the practice test is just that: practice. Memorizing these questions and answers will not be very helpful on the actual test because it is unlikely to have any of the same exact questions. If you only know the right answers to the sample questions, you won't be prepared for the real thing. **Study the concepts** until you understand them fully, and then you'll be able to answer any question that shows up on the test.

It's important to wait on the practice tests until you're ready. If you take a test on your first day of study, you may be overwhelmed by the amount of material covered and how much you need to learn. Work up to it gradually.

On test day, you'll need to be prepared for answering questions, managing your time, and using the test-taking strategies you've learned. It's a lot to balance, like a mental marathon that will have a big impact on your future. Like training for a marathon, you'll need to start slowly and work your way up. When test day arrives, you'll be ready.

Start with the strategies you've read in the first two Secret Keys—plan your course and study in the way that works best for you. If you have time, consider using multiple study resources to get different approaches to the same concepts. It can be helpful to see difficult concepts from more than one angle. Then find a good source for practice tests. Many times, the test website will suggest potential study resources or provide sample tests.

Practice Test Strategy

When you're ready to start taking practice tests, follow this strategy:

Untimed and Open-Book Practice

Take the first test with no time constraints and with your notes and study guide handy. Take your time and focus on applying the strategies you've learned.

Timed and Open-Book Practice

Take the second practice test open-book as well, but set a timer and practice pacing yourself to finish in time.

Timed and Closed-Book Practice

Take any other practice tests as if it were test day. Set a timer and put away your study materials. Sit at a table or desk in a quiet room, imagine yourself at the testing center, and answer questions as quickly and accurately as possible.

Keep repeating timed and closed-book tests on a regular basis until you run out of practice tests or it's time for the actual test. Your mind will be ready for the schedule and stress of test day, and you'll be able to focus on recalling the material you've learned.

Secret Key #4 – Pace Yourself

Once you're fully prepared for the material on the test, your biggest challenge on test day will be managing your time. Just knowing that the clock is ticking can make you panic even if you have plenty of time left. Work on pacing yourself so you can build confidence against the time constraints of the exam. Pacing is a difficult skill to master, especially in a high-pressure environment, so **practice is vital**.

Set time expectations for your pace based on how much time is available. For example, if a section has 60 questions and the time limit is 30 minutes, you know you have to average 30 seconds or less per question in order to answer them all. Although 30 seconds is the hard limit, set 25 seconds per question as your goal, so you reserve extra time to spend on harder questions. When you budget extra time for the harder questions, you no longer have any reason to stress when those questions take longer to answer.

Don't let this time expectation distract you from working through the test at a calm, steady pace, but keep it in mind so you don't spend too much time on any one question. Recognize that taking extra time on one question you don't understand may keep you from answering two that you do understand later in the test. If your time limit for a question is up and you're still not sure of the answer, mark it and move on, and come back to it later if the time and the test format allow. If the testing format doesn't allow you to return to earlier questions, just make an educated guess; then put it out of your mind and move on.

On the easier questions, be careful not to rush. It may seem wise to hurry through them so you have more time for the challenging ones, but it's not worth missing one if you know the concept and just didn't take the time to read the question fully. Work efficiently but make sure you understand the question and have looked at all of the answer choices, since more than one may seem right at first.

Even if you're paying attention to the time, you may find yourself a little behind at some point. You should speed up to get back on track, but do so wisely. Don't panic; just take a few seconds less on each question until you're caught up. Don't guess without thinking, but do look through the answer choices and eliminate any you know are wrong. If you can get down to two choices, it is often worthwhile to guess from those. Once you've chosen an answer, move on and don't dwell on any that you skipped or had to hurry through. If a question was taking too long, chances are it was one of the harder ones, so you weren't as likely to get it right anyway.

On the other hand, if you find yourself getting ahead of schedule, it may be beneficial to slow down a little. The more quickly you work, the more likely you are to make a careless mistake that will affect your score. You've budgeted time for each question, so don't be afraid to spend that time. Practice an efficient but careful pace to get the most out of the time you have.

Secret Key #5 – Have a Plan for Guessing

When you're taking the test, you may find yourself stuck on a question. Some of the answer choices seem better than others, but you don't see the one answer choice that is obviously correct. What do you do?

The scenario described above is very common, yet most test takers have not effectively prepared for it. Developing and practicing a plan for guessing may be one of the single most effective uses of your time as you get ready for the exam.

In developing your plan for guessing, there are three questions to address:

- When should you start the guessing process?
- How should you narrow down the choices?
- Which answer should you choose?

When to Start the Guessing Process

Unless your plan for guessing is to select C every time (which, despite its merits, is not what we recommend), you need to leave yourself enough time to apply your answer elimination strategies. Since you have a limited amount of time for each question, that means that if you're going to give yourself the best shot at guessing correctly, you have to decide quickly whether or not you will guess.

Of course, the best-case scenario is that you don't have to guess at all, so first, see if you can answer the question based on your knowledge of the subject and basic reasoning skills. Focus on the key words in the question and try to jog your memory of related topics. Give yourself a chance to bring the knowledge to mind, but once you realize that you don't have (or you can't access) the knowledge you need to answer the question, it's time to start the guessing process.

It's almost always better to start the guessing process too early than too late. It only takes a few seconds to remember something and answer the question from knowledge. Carefully eliminating wrong answer choices takes longer. Plus, going through the process of eliminating answer choices can actually help jog your memory.

Summary: Start the guessing process as soon as you decide that you can't answer the question based on your knowledge.

How to Narrow Down the Choices

The next chapter in this book (**Test-Taking Strategies**) includes a wide range of strategies for how to approach questions and how to look for answer choices to eliminate. You will definitely want to read those carefully, practice them, and figure out which ones work best for you. Here though, we're going to address a mindset rather than a particular strategy.

Your chances of guessing an answer correctly depend on how many options you are choosing from.

How many choices you have	How likely you are to guess correctly
5	20%
4	25%
3	33%
2	50%
1	100%

You can see from this chart just how valuable it is to be able to eliminate incorrect answers and make an educated guess, but there are two things that many test takers do that cause them to miss out on the benefits of guessing:

- Accidentally eliminating the correct answer
- Selecting an answer based on an impression

We'll look at the first one here, and the second one in the next section.

To avoid accidentally eliminating the correct answer, we recommend a thought exercise called **the $5 challenge**. In this challenge, you only eliminate an answer choice from contention if you are willing to bet $5 on it being wrong. Why $5? Five dollars is a small but not insignificant amount of money. It's an amount you could afford to lose but wouldn't want to throw away. And while losing $5 once might not hurt too much, doing it twenty times will set you back $100. In the same way, each small decision you make—eliminating a choice here, guessing on a question there—won't by itself impact your score very much, but when you put them all together, they can make a big difference. By holding each answer choice elimination decision to a higher standard, you can reduce the risk of accidentally eliminating the correct answer.

The $5 challenge can also be applied in a positive sense: If you are willing to bet $5 that an answer choice *is* correct, go ahead and mark it as correct.

Summary: Only eliminate an answer choice if you are willing to bet $5 that it is wrong.

Which Answer to Choose

You're taking the test. You've run into a hard question and decided you'll have to guess. You've eliminated all the answer choices you're willing to bet $5 on. Now you have to pick an answer. Why do we even need to talk about this? Why can't you just pick whichever one you feel like when the time comes?

The answer to these questions is that if you don't come into the test with a plan, you'll rely on your impression to select an answer choice, and if you do that, you risk falling into a trap. The test writers know that everyone who takes their test will be guessing on some of the questions, so they intentionally write wrong answer choices to seem plausible. You still have to pick an answer though, and if the wrong answer choices are designed to look right, how can you ever be sure that you're not falling for their trap? The best solution we've found to this dilemma is to take the decision out of your hands entirely. Here is the process we recommend:

Once you've eliminated any choices that you are confident (willing to bet $5) are wrong, select the first remaining choice as your answer.

Whether you choose to select the first remaining choice, the second, or the last, the important thing is that you use some preselected standard. Using this approach guarantees that you will not be enticed into selecting an answer choice that looks right, because you are not basing your decision on how the answer choices look.

This is not meant to make you question your knowledge. Instead, it is to help you recognize the difference between your knowledge and your impressions. There's a huge difference between thinking an answer is right because of what you know, and thinking an answer is right because it looks or sounds like it should be right.

Summary: To ensure that your selection is appropriately random, make a predetermined selection from among all answer choices you have not eliminated.

Test-Taking Strategies

This section contains a list of test-taking strategies that you may find helpful as you work through the test. By taking what you know and applying logical thought, you can maximize your chances of answering any question correctly!

It is very important to realize that every question is different and every person is different: no single strategy will work on every question, and no single strategy will work for every person. That's why we've included all of them here, so you can try them out and determine which ones work best for different types of questions and which ones work best for you.

Question Strategies

Read Carefully

Read the question and answer choices carefully. Don't miss the question because you misread the terms. You have plenty of time to read each question thoroughly and make sure you understand what is being asked. Yet a happy medium must be attained, so don't waste too much time. You must read carefully, but efficiently.

Contextual Clues

Look for contextual clues. If the question includes a word you are not familiar with, look at the immediate context for some indication of what the word might mean. Contextual clues can often give you all the information you need to decipher the meaning of an unfamiliar word. Even if you can't determine the meaning, you may be able to narrow down the possibilities enough to make a solid guess at the answer to the question.

Prefixes

If you're having trouble with a word in the question or answer choices, try dissecting it. Take advantage of every clue that the word might include. Prefixes and suffixes can be a huge help. Usually they allow you to determine a basic meaning. Pre- means before, post- means after, pro - is positive, de- is negative. From prefixes and suffixes, you can get an idea of the general meaning of the word and try to put it into context.

Hedge Words

Watch out for critical hedge words, such as *likely, may, can, sometimes, often, almost, mostly, usually, generally, rarely,* and *sometimes.* Question writers insert these hedge phrases to cover every possibility. Often an answer choice will be wrong simply because it leaves no room for exception. Be on guard for answer choices that have definitive words such as *exactly* and *always.*

Switchback Words

Stay alert for *switchbacks*. These are the words and phrases frequently used to alert you to shifts in thought. The most common switchback words are *but, although,* and *however.* Others include *nevertheless, on the other hand, even though, while, in spite of, despite, regardless of.* Switchback words are important to catch because they can change the direction of the question or an answer choice.

Face Value

When in doubt, use common sense. Accept the situation in the problem at face value. Don't read too much into it. These problems will not require you to make wild assumptions. If you have to go beyond creativity and warp time or space in order to have an answer choice fit the question, then you should move on and consider the other answer choices. These are normal problems rooted in reality. The applicable relationship or explanation may not be readily apparent, but it is there for you to figure out. Use your common sense to interpret anything that isn't clear.

Answer Choice Strategies

Answer Selection

The most thorough way to pick an answer choice is to identify and eliminate wrong answers until only one is left, then confirm it is the correct answer. Sometimes an answer choice may immediately seem right, but be careful. The test writers will usually put more than one reasonable answer choice on each question, so take a second to read all of them and make sure that the other choices are not equally obvious. As long as you have time left, it is better to read every answer choice than to pick the first one that looks right without checking the others.

Answer Choice Families

An answer choice family consists of two (in rare cases, three) answer choices that are very similar in construction and cannot all be true at the same time. If you see two answer choices that are direct opposites or parallels, one of them is usually the correct answer. For instance, if one answer choice says that quantity *x* increases and another either says that quantity *x* decreases (opposite) or says that quantity *y* increases (parallel), then those answer choices would fall into the same family. An answer choice that doesn't match the construction of the answer choice family is more likely to be incorrect. Most questions will not have answer choice families, but when they do appear, you should be prepared to recognize them.

Eliminate Answers

Eliminate answer choices as soon as you realize they are wrong, but make sure you consider all possibilities. If you are eliminating answer choices and realize that the last one you are left with is also wrong, don't panic. Start over and consider each choice again. There may be something you missed the first time that you will realize on the second pass.

Avoid Fact Traps

Don't be distracted by an answer choice that is factually true but doesn't answer the question. You are looking for the choice that answers the question. Stay focused on what the question is asking for so you don't accidentally pick an answer that is true but incorrect. Always go back to the question and make sure the answer choice you've selected actually answers the question and is not merely a true statement.

Extreme Statements

In general, you should avoid answers that put forth extreme actions as standard practice or proclaim controversial ideas as established fact. An answer choice that states the "process should be used in certain situations, if..." is much more likely to be correct than one that states the "process should be discontinued completely." The first is a calm rational statement and doesn't even make a definitive, uncompromising stance, using a hedge word *if* to provide wiggle room, whereas the second choice is a radical idea and far more extreme.

Benchmark

As you read through the answer choices and you come across one that seems to answer the question well, mentally select that answer choice. This is not your final answer, but it's the one that will help you evaluate the other answer choices. The one that you selected is your benchmark or standard for judging each of the other answer choices. Every other answer choice must be compared to your benchmark. That choice is correct until proven otherwise by another answer choice beating it. If you find a better answer, then that one becomes your new benchmark. Once you've decided that no other choice answers the question as well as your benchmark, you have your final answer.

Predict the Answer

Before you even start looking at the answer choices, it is often best to try to predict the answer. When you come up with the answer on your own, it is easier to avoid distractions and traps because you will know exactly what to look for. The right answer choice is unlikely to be word-for-word what you came up with, but it should be a close match. Even if you are confident that you have the right answer, you should still take the time to read each option before moving on.

General Strategies

Tough Questions

If you are stumped on a problem or it appears too hard or too difficult, don't waste time. Move on! Remember though, if you can quickly check for obviously incorrect answer choices, your chances of guessing correctly are greatly improved. Before you completely give up, at least try to knock out a couple of possible answers. Eliminate what you can and then guess at the remaining answer choices before moving on.

Check Your Work

Since you will probably not know every term listed and the answer to every question, it is important that you get credit for the ones that you do know. Don't miss any questions through careless mistakes. If at all possible, try to take a second to look back over your answer selection and make sure you've selected the correct answer choice and haven't made a costly careless mistake (such as marking an answer choice that you didn't mean to mark). This quick double check should more than pay for itself in caught mistakes for the time it costs.

Pace Yourself

It's easy to be overwhelmed when you're looking at a page full of questions; your mind is confused and full of random thoughts, and the clock is ticking down faster than you would like. Calm down and maintain the pace that you have set for yourself. Especially as you get down to the last few minutes of the test, don't let the small numbers on the clock make you panic. As long as you are on track by monitoring your pace, you are guaranteed to have time for each question.

Don't Rush

It is very easy to make errors when you are in a hurry. Maintaining a fast pace in answering questions is pointless if it makes you miss questions that you would have gotten right otherwise. Test writers like to include distracting information and wrong answers that seem right. Taking a little extra time to avoid careless mistakes can make all the difference in your test score. Find a pace that allows you to be confident in the answers that you select.

Keep Moving

Panicking will not help you pass the test, so do your best to stay calm and keep moving. Taking deep breaths and going through the answer elimination steps you practiced can help to break through a stress barrier and keep your pace.

Final Notes

The combination of a solid foundation of content knowledge and the confidence that comes from practicing your plan for applying that knowledge is the key to maximizing your performance on test day. As your foundation of content knowledge is built up and strengthened, you'll find that the strategies included in this chapter become more and more effective in helping you quickly sift through the distractions and traps of the test to isolate the correct answer.

Now it's time to move on to the test content chapters of this book, but be sure to keep your goal in mind. As you read, think about how you will be able to apply this information on the test. If you've already seen sample questions for the test and you have an idea of the question format and style, try to come up with questions of your own that you can answer based on what you're reading. This will give you valuable practice applying your knowledge in the same ways you can expect to on test day.

Good luck and good studying!

Functional Anatomy and Exercise Physiology

Biomechanics, kinetics, and kinematics

The three fields of study of biomechanics, kinetics, and kinematics help the exercise specialist to learn a great deal about human motion and its causes. This knowledge can help the exercise specialist in many ways.

First, by understanding the forces that act upon a human body to create motion, the exercise specialist can better understand the impact of different exercises on the body and develop an exercise program that both is appropriate to an individual's needs and reduces the risks of injury.

Second, by understanding how the body moves during different activities, the exercise specialist is able to teach the ideal way to perform different movements and activities. This reduces the risks of injury. The exercise specialist will also be better able to identify abnormalities of gait and motion, which may help to diagnose more serious issues.

<u>Walking, jogging, and running</u>

The typical walk involves the stride of the legs and swing of the arms. Each step begins with the heel coming into contact with the ground first. Then the foot rolls into a flat position. At this point the weight is distributed evenly between the two feet. The heel of the trailing foot then lifts off the ground, followed by the toe. That foot then becomes the lead foot and the cycle repeats. The arms swing opposite to the legs, with the left arm coming forward as the right foot makes contact with the ground. Most adults walk at a speed around three miles per hour.

Jogging and running require more balance and more strength than walking. They also demand a greater range of motion. The driving force is more horizontal than it is for walking, the stride is longer, and the body leans slightly forward.

Muscle weakness and neurological disorders can create an abnormal gait.

<u>Weight lifting and in lifting</u>

When lifting or moving heavy objects, it is important that the body be close to the object. Just like the human body, the object has a center of gravity. Bring the body's center of gravity as close as possible to the object's center of gravity. Use a wide stance to increase stability. The person lifting should use care not to twist when lifting a heavy object. The majority of the lifting should be done with the muscles in the legs rather than those of the back.

When carrying a heavy object, a person should keep its center of gravity close to his own. Pushing, pulling, rolling, or sliding a heavy object is better than lifting and carrying it—these actions have a lower risk of injury.

<u>Swimming and cycling</u>

During swimming, the body's natural buoyancy combines with strokes and kicks to move the body through the water. The individual level of buoyancy depends on the relative amounts of body fat, bone, and muscle. Higher bone and muscle mass result in less buoyancy. When a person swims, the arm strokes and leg kicks that she uses should help to move her forward through the water. Side-to-side movements should be kept to a minimum. The water provides resistance, which increases the challenge of the activity.

During cycling, proper balance, posture, and pedaling action are all important. The action of pedaling is timed a bit like walking. When one foot reaches the height of the pedal circle, that foot applies pressure to move the pedal forward. At the bottom of the circle, the foot rests until it reaches the top again. In this way, the feet and legs alternate between resting and pushing.

When a person goes from a state of rest to one of light exertion, a number of metabolic changes occur. To begin with, she begins to breathe more rapidly in order to bring more oxygen to the cells and tissues. With light exertion, the breathing rate usually normalizes within 4 minutes. Once the uptake reaches a steady state, the exercise becomes aerobic in nature.

Until oxygen uptake normalizes, the body depends on anaerobic energy sources. During the beginning of muscle work, the body relies on the creatine phosphate system and rapid glycolysis to produce the ATP that muscles need. During the transition from a resting state to light exertion, glycogen serves as the body's primary fuel source for the muscles.

Measuring

Most often the body's metabolism is measured either through direct or indirect calorimetry. The calories a person consumes and the oxygen that he breathes are converted to heat and also exhaled as carbon dioxide and water vapor. By measuring a body's heat production, you can learn about the body's metabolic rate. You can measure it precisely by placing the patient in an airtight chamber and measuring the heat change in the chamber. This method is not always practical.

An indirect measurement can be made by determining the patient's level of oxygen consumption (VO_2). You can then calculate metabolism by using the following equation:

$$\text{Metabolic Rate}(\text{kcal} - \text{min}^{-1}) = VO_2\ (\text{L} - \text{min}^{-1}) \times [4.0 + \text{RQ}]$$

High-intensity versus ongoing submaximal exercise

When a person exercises in short bursts of high intensity—weight-lifting or sprinting, for example—the body uses anaerobic systems in order to provide the body's fuel. The ATP production for very short bursts of energy lasting under five seconds usually depends on the creatine phosphate system. Longer, high-intensity bursts tap into glycolysis to produce ATP. The metabolism doesn't shift abruptly from one system to the other. Rather there is a slow shift so that both systems are engaged at the same time for a period.

During longer, submaximal exercise that lasts for 10 minutes or more, the body begins to draw from carbohydrate and fat sources for fuel. The ATP production is done through the aerobic metabolism.

Aerobic and anaerobic metabolism

The foundation of muscle metabolism is the production of adenosine triphosphate (ATP). Aerobic oxidation is one mechanism the body uses in the production of ATP. The two other methods are creatine phosphate and rapid glycolysis (both anaerobic).

Anaerobic metabolism decreases as an activity goes on. It increases when an activity becomes more intense. Aerobic metabolism takes place during longer activities of a lower intensity.

Anaerobic energy production relies primarily on carbohydrates for fuel, while aerobic energy production shifts to a reliance on fat stored in the body when exercise lasts more than 30 minutes.

Anaerobic threshold

At the anaerobic threshold, the body's energy demands surpass the ability of the circulation system to keep up with aerobic metabolism. The anaerobic threshold can be measured by measuring exhaled gases during exercise. To measure anaerobic response, the level of pulmonary ventilation (V_E) and the level of carbon dioxide (VCO_2) are measured during exercise. There is a point when the level of these gases outpaces the increase in exercise intensity. This is the threshold point. Usually the anaerobic threshold is stated as a percentage of the individual's maximum oxygen capacity. For instance, an individual might reach his anaerobic threshold at 75% of his maximum oxygen capacity. This means that the individual should be able to work out at 75% of his maximum capacity without relying on anaerobic metabolism. In this manner, the onset of muscle fatigue can be delayed. A typical individual has an anaerobic threshold between 47 and 64 percent of maximum capacity. This number rises physical condition improves.

Energy cost

The energy cost of an activity is the number of calories it burns during a set course of time. More intense activities have a higher energy cost. Doing an activity for a longer period of time also leads to a higher energy cost. Activities that challenge larger groups of muscles like those in the back and legs also generate a higher energy costs. The term metabolic equivalent is sometimes used to describe the level of intensity associated with exercise. It is described as a unit measure—MET. The base MET unit is equal to the energy cost during a minute of rest for the average person. So an activity that is 5 METs has five times the energy cost of resting. Some common activities and their associated METs are bicycling (8.0 MET), Step Aerobics (10.0 MET), golf (4.5 MET), basketball (6.0 MET), and running at a 5 mile per hour pace (8.0 MET).

Pulse rate

By taking a measure of the pulse, the exercise specialist can measure a patient's heart rate, which can reveal much about the patient's health. You can measure the pulse by applying pressure with your finger along a large- or medium-sized artery. The most common places to take the pulse are along the carotid artery, the brachial artery, or the radial artery. The carotid artery is in the neck and is located next to the trachea. You can feel it below the jaw, just to the side of the larynx. The brachial artery is found in the upper arm toward the inside of the body. You can feel it between the bicep and triceps or in medial side of front of the elbow (the bend). The radial artery can be found on the inside of the wrist, just above the thumb.

Heart beats

Unlike other muscles in the body, the heart's regular contractions are not triggered by signals from the brain. Cardiac cells, called intercalated discs, run end-to-end within the heart. The interconnectivity of the cells makes it possible for an electrical impulse to travel through the cells. The sinoatrial (SA) node spontaneously releases an electrical impulse every second or so. The impulse moves from cell to cell through the atria until it reaches the atriovenntricular (AV) node. This causes the atria to contract. The impulse then moves through the ventricles. Factors outside the heart can influence the force with which it beats, and how fast the SA node triggers it to beat. Some of these factors include hormone levels and nerve control.

Maximal oxygen consumption

Maximal oxygen consumption is the most accepted way to measure a person's cardiovascular fitness. It is a physical measure of the highest level of oxygen transport when a patient is exerting herself at her physical limit. It is calculated as the product of the heart rate, stroke volume, and arteriovenous oxygen difference. Usually, the maximal oxygen consumption is measured by assessing the volume and level of oxygen in a person's exhaled air. The result must be adjusted to a standard

temperature and pressure. There are a variety of exercise tests that can either measure or estimate the maximal oxygen consumption. The Douglas bag technique is one. Another is the Bruce test.

Measuring

Myocardial oxygen consumption refers to the actual oxygen used by the heart. The heart rate, the rate and strength of contraction of the heart muscle, and the amount of tension in the ventricular wall all contribute to the myocardial oxygen consumption. When someone begins to exercise, the increase in heart rate is the main cause of higher myocardial oxygen consumption. Increased blood flow helps to meet the higher demand. For people with ischemic heart disease, high rates of exertion can lead to chest pains. When this occurs, it usually means that the heart's demand for oxygen has exceeded the available supply.

Center of gravity

The center of gravity is considered to be the point at the center of the body's mass. It is usually positioned between the iliac crests. The feet form the base of support. A person can lower his center of gravity by bending his knees, and can increase his base of support by widening his stance. These two adjustments increase the body's stability. Stability and balance combine to help keep a person on his feet despite movements or impacts, both expected and unexpected. In other words, a person with greater stability and balance is harder to knock down and less likely to fall down. Proper spinal alignment is important. It keeps the center of gravity centered in the sagittal plane, makes the base of support more stable, and increases overall balance and stability.

Force

The laws of inertia, acceleration, and reaction are laws first identified by Isaac Newton in order to describe the interactions between objects and the forces that act upon them. A force is any push, pull, or other action that can potentially change the motion of a mass.

The first law is the law of inertia. This law states that objects resist change. That means that an object in motion will stay in motion if no outside forces act upon it. Likewise, an object at rest will stay at rest unless a force is applied to it.

The second law of thermodynamics is the law of acceleration. It states that the acceleration (i.e. change in motion) will be related directly to and occur in the direction of the force applied to the object. There is also an inverse relationship between acceleration and the mass of the object in question.

The third law, the law of reaction, is commonly expressed as, "For every action there is an equal and opposite reaction."

Primary forces that affect a body's movement

The three primary forces that affect a body's movement are the ground reaction force, the frictional force, and the muscular force.

When a person stands on the ground, the weight of her body applies a force against the ground. In accordance with Newton's third law, the ground also applies an equal and opposite force against the person's feet. This is the ground reaction force. Furthermore, when a person pushes off against the ground, the resulting force makes movement by walking or running possible.

Whenever two bodies come into contact, such as a foot coming into contact with the ground, there is also a frictional force that is generated.

Finally, muscle movements apply forces to various body parts moving them in different ways.

Translatory motion

When a force is applied to an object that is free to move in a linear or curved path, the resulting motion is said to be translatory. This term also is used to describe the kind of motion that occurs when a force is applied to the object's center.

When a force is applied to object that is free to move in a rotational path (such as a circle or an orbit), the resulting motion is said to be rotary. This term also is used to describe the kind of motion that occurs when a force is applied to an object away from the object's center.

Velocity describes the distance an object travels in a measured period of time. It is always measured in distance over time, as for instance in meters per second or miles per hour.

Momentum is determined by multiplying the moving object's mass by its velocity.

Levers

Levers are an important concept to the exercise specialist because they come into play when teaching a patient how to properly lift weights or move heavy objects. A lever uses a rigid bar and a fulcrum to reduce the amount of force needed to move an object. There are three classes of levers. A first-class lever has an axis (fulcrum) situated at any point between two arms. Force is applied to one arm in order to move the other. A second-class lever has the axis at one end. The force arm has the greater length of the two arms. A third class lever also has the axis at one end, but the force arm is shorter. A shovel is an example of third-class lever. The top hand serves as the axis. The distance between the two hands is the length of the force arm. The distance between the axis and shovelhead is the length of the other arm (often called the resistance arm).

Muscle fatigue

Muscle fatigue occurs when a person exercises his muscles to the point of exhaustion. When an individual performs strength-training exercises to the point where the muscles begin to lose power and performance begins to fall, he has reached muscle fatigue. Doing strength-training exercises to the point of muscle fatigue is one way to develop muscle strength.

Even in someone with well-trained muscles, muscle soreness can result after exercises that work the muscles in a new way or after sessions that are especially intense. This is often referred to as delayed onset muscle soreness and is characterized by soreness that sets in up to 48 hours after exercise and lasts up to 10 days.

Fatigue

There are several factors that contribute to the fatigue associated with long periods of aerobic activity. During exercise, glycogen is often used as a fuel source. It is stored in the muscles and liver for the body to access when needed. During long bouts of exercise these stores can become depleted. Exercise also uses blood glucose as fuel. After a prolonged period of activity, blood glucose levels can fall enough to cause a decrease in energy. Exertion depletes the body's fluids, so dehydration is often a factor in fatigue. Also, the body's temperature begins to rise during exercise, and this can affect energy levels as well.

It may be that periodically eating small amounts of carbohydrates during long periods of exercise can help to reduce depletion of glycogen and blood glucose.

Heat stress

Temperature is an important consideration when it comes to physical exertion. Exercise can alter a person's body temperature. Environmental factors can also affect body temperature. As an exercise specialist, you should plan to advise your patients about monitoring their temperature.

The primary cause of heat gain during exercise is actual energy metabolism. Increased metabolism during exercise releases more heat through muscle contractions. The body balances this by sweating, a process which helps to cool the body. The type of clothing a person wears can inhibit this cooling process. Advise your patients to wear light clothing that breathes easily. Advise your patients to take extra precautions when exercising on a hot day. They should drink more water and take regular breaks to self-monitor. If they feel fatigued or dizzy, they should rest in a cool place.

Heat-related disorders

Heat cramps cause involuntary contractions in the abdominal or other fatigued muscles. The cramps are quite painful, and usually signal an electrolyte imbalance in the body. The person experiencing cramps should rest in a cool place and drink a glass of lightly salted water.

Heat syncope causes blurry vision or vision that seems gray. It can cause fainting spells. The best solution is to rest in a cool place. The person should lie down.

Dehydration can lead to fatigue, a dry feeling in the mouth, and weakness. It's important for the dehydrated person to drink plenty of water. Lightly salted water or a sports drink with electrolytes can also be beneficial.

Heat exhaustion is a more serious condition that can cause fatigue, dizziness, and headaches. It can also cause low blood pressure and fainting. Resting in a cool environment and drinking plenty of water should remedy the condition.

Heat stroke is a very serious condition that can cause a fever, disorientation, and unconsciousness. It requires immediate cooling and, occasionally, a visit to the hospital.

Cold stress

Exercising in cold temperatures can stress the body in different ways than exercising in warm temperatures. Cold stress occurs when the person exercising loses more heat through convection, radiation, evaporation, or conduction than they produce through the higher energy metabolism of exercise. Cold stress is more likely to occur when an individual exercises to the point of fatigue.

As an exercise specialist, you should advise your patients to take precautions when exercising in the cold. The main precaution is to dress properly. When exercising at temperatures at or below freezing, recommend that your patients wear proper layers to help insulate against the cold. Because conditions like frostbite and frost nip typically affect the extremities, proper socks and gloves are especially important.

Cold-related disorders

- Hypothermia is a condition that occurs in degrees. Mild hypothermia may lead to chills and fatigue. Serious hypothermia can lead to pain in the arms and legs. It can cause the body's core temperature to drop to 95 degrees Fahrenheit or lower. It can lead to weakness, disorientation, and unconsciousness. When someone suffers from hypothermia, remove any wet clothing and get him somewhere warm. Give him something warm and non-alcoholic to drink. Serious cases require hospitalization.
- Frostbite affects the extremities, usually fingers, toes or feet. Early signs are a burning sensation, followed by numbness or tingling. The skin may blister and become red, gray, white, or black. Treat a person with frostbite like you would someone with hypothermia. Treat the affected area like a burn. Serious frostbite requires hospital care.
- With frost nip, the skin turns white and itches. Treatment is the same as for frostbite.
- Trench foot causes severe pain and blisters. It also is treated like frostbite.

High altitude illnesses

Higher altitudes have lower oxygen levels. Exertion at a higher altitude can lead to altitude-related illnesses. Some potential conditions are acute mountain sickness, high altitude pulmonary edema and high altitude cerebral edema. Acute mountain sickness triggers headaches, nausea, low appetite, fatigue, and difficulty sleeping. High altitude pulmonary edema leads to a buildup of fluid in the pulmonary system. It usually presents with chest pains, and sometimes an irregular heart beat. A cerebral edema is a buildup of fluid in the brain. It presents with the same symptoms as acute mountain sickness accompanied by changes in mental state. If an edema occurs, the person must be moved to a lower altitude immediately and should receive medical care. Slowing the ascent rate, eating more carbohydrates, drinking plenty of water and supplementing with gingko biloba can all help prevent altitude sickness. Also refrain from overexertion while adjusting to new altitudes.

Air pollution

Contaminants in the air can affect exercise performance and endurance. Outdoor pollution commonly contains the byproducts of industrial activities, including factory outputs and outputs from vehicles. Indoor pollution can also be a problem. There are two categories of pollutants. Primary pollutants come directly from an identifiable source. Secondary pollutants are the product of reactions between pollutants and other things, like moisture or sunlight. Pollution can irritate the airways and lungs, making it more difficult to breath. It can also affect the air-gas exchange that happens in the lungs, which may reduce the amount of oxygen reaching the tissues. You should advise your patients to monitor air quality in their area if it is a concern. Encourage them to participate in outdoor activities when local meteorologists measure pollution concentration at or below 100.

Important Terms

Inferior: In terms of anatomy, inferior refers to a lower position in the body, a position that is closer to the feet. For example, the knee is inferior to the hip.

Superior: Superior refers to a higher location in the body, a position that is closer to the head. For example, the lungs are superior to the liver.

Medial: Medial is used in two ways in reference to anatomy. First, it refers to being toward the middle. In the instance of the knee, the inside of the knee is referred to as the medial side. When dealing with a structure that has layers, the middle layer is often called the medial layer.

Lateral: Lateral means toward the outside or away from the middle. The outside of the knee is the lateral side, for example.

Supination: This term refers to the position of the arm/hand or the leg/foot such that the palm or the sole is facing up.

Pronation: This term refers to the position of the arm/hand or the leg/foot such that the palm or the sole is facing down.

Flexion: This is a technical term referring to the action of bending. Flexion of the toes, for example, would mean curling.

Extension: This is a technical term referring to the action of straightening a joint or joints. A person uses the extension of the leg and hip to move to a standing position.

Adduction: This term refers to movement that is toward the middle of the body. It is often used to describe muscles that pull toward the body's midline.

Abduction: This term refers to movement that is away from the middle of the body. It is often used to describe muscles that pull away from the body's midline.

Hyperextension: This refers to the act of extending a muscle, tendon, or ligament beyond its natural range of motion. Hyperextension usually results in an injury.

Rotation: This term refers to the act of moving around a central axis and often describes the specific movement of joints.

Circumduction: This describes one of four possible types of joint movement. In this kind of joint, the head of one long bone connects with an articular cavity of another bone.

Agonist: This describes the muscle that is primarily responsible for a movement. During a bicep curl, the bicep muscle is one of the agonist muscles.

Antagonist: During any motion, there is also an opposing group of muscles. These are called the antagonist muscles. In the case of a bicep curl, the triceps acts as an antagonist muscle.

Stabilizer: During many motions, there are also muscles that help to reduce unwanted movement. These are called stabilizer muscles.

Contractile Proteins: The cells within the muscles contain the contractile proteins, actin and myosin. These two proteins interact to cause the muscle to contract, enabling movement.

Regulatory Proteins: The cells within the muscles also contain the proteins troponin and tropomyosin. These two chemicals bind actin and myosin, inhibiting muscle contractions and causing the muscles to relax.

Respiratory Membrane: Within the lungs are the alveoli. The alveoli and the capillaries exchange gases. The alveoli pass oxygen into the capillaries, oxygenating the blood, and the capillaries pass carbon dioxide into the alveoli where it can be exhaled out of the body. This exchange of gases occurs through the respiratory membrane that separates the alveoli from the capillaries.

Buoyancy: Many types of objects, including the human body, tend to float when submerged in a liquid. This tendency is called buoyancy.

Drag: When a body moves through a liquid, the liquid exerts a force in the opposite direction of movement. This force is called drag.

Force: A force is any action that works to change the motion of an object. Often a force can be thought of as a push or a pull. (A force can also change an object's shape).

Friction: Whenever two surfaces in contact move against each other, a force is created and works against the movement. This force is friction.

Lift: When a body moves through a liquid, there is a force that acts perpendicular to the flow of the liquid around the body. This force is called lift.

Kinematics: This is the scientific study of the mechanics of movement and motion.

Kinetics: This is the scientific study of the mechanics responsible for movement and motion. Kinetics and kinematics are closely related fields of study.

Normal Reaction: When two surfaces are in contact they exert equal and opposite forces against each other. This is known as the normal reaction.

Stiffness: Different materials have different levels of elasticity. Stiffness is how elasticity is measured. The stiffness of a material is defined using a graph of the stress versus the strain. The stiffness is the slope.

Strain: When an object is acted on by a force, the force may change the motion and/or the shape of the object. When the shape is changed, the strain measures the amount of deformation.

Stress: This is a measure of the force applied per area. For example, when a force is applied to a surface measured in square inches, the force would be the strain per square inch.

Torque: When a force moves an object around an axis, it is often referred to as having a rotating effect. This rotating effect is also called torque.

Vector: A vector describes a force. It is treated as a variable and both the magnitude of the force and its direction must be known to define the vector.

Acute Mountain Sickness: When the human body experiences a sudden gain in elevation the differences in air pressure and the oxygen content of the air can lead to headaches, nausea, and fatigue.

Central Fatigue: As the human body exercises, it becomes more and more tired. When this happens, the response of motor neurons becomes slower. This is referred to as central fatigue.

Cold Stress: When the body begins to lose heat either from the core or from the extremities due to the environment, changes in metabolism, or improper clothing, it puts a strain on the body. This is known as cold stress.

Energy Metabolism: The body depends on the production of adenosine triphosphate to trigger muscle contractions. The energy metabolism is the overall effect of the reactions that produce this compound.

Progressive Resistance describes the process of giving muscles an increased challenge in each workout, so that the muscles begin to grow stronger. There are several ways to implement progressive resistance—greater weight, more repetitions, slower movements.

Isotonic or isometric exercises involve contracting muscles without moving them through a range of motion. An example is pushing the palms of the hands together in front of the body.

Concentric exercises are those in which the muscle length decreases during contraction.

Eccentric exercises are those in which the muscle length increases during contraction.

Plyometrics use sudden bursts of rapid muscle movement to build strength for athletic movements like jumping or punching.

Atrophy: Muscles must be used in order to stay strong. During a long period of no use, muscles may become smaller, a process known as atrophy.

Hypertrophy: When the cells of an organ or muscle grow in size without increasing in number, it is referred to as hypertrophy. Strength training can cause visible bulking of the muscles, referred to as muscular hypertrophy.

Sets and Repetitions: When lifting weights, it is common practice to do a specific number of sets, each containing a specific number of repetitions of the movement in question.

Valsalva maneuver: Plugging the nose and sealing the lips while exhaling forces air through the Eustacian tube and into the ear. Because the action of exhaling in this manner increases pressure in the chest and increases blood pressure slightly, the maneuver can be used to test cardiac function.

Trapezius: This muscle is located in the upper back, extending from the neck to the mid-point between the neck and shoulder and down to the middle of the back.

Pectoralis Major: This is the primary muscle in the upper chest. It originates at the sternum and stretches across the chest to the side of the body.

Latissimus Dorsi: This muscle is located in the middle back and helps with some movements of the arms and shoulders.

Biceps: These muscles are located in the upper front of each arm. They help to bend the arm.

Triceps: The triceps are located in the upper back of each arm. They help with arm extension.

Rectus Abdominis: The rectus abdominis is located in the abdomen. It extends from the diaphragm to the base of the pelvis. It helps when bending forward and plays a role in exhalation.

Internal and External Obliques: The oblique muscles are the primary abdominal muscles located on the sides of the body. They extend from the top of the hip to the base of the pectoral muscles.

Erector Spinae: Located in the back, this muscle originates from the sacrum and extends up to the thoracic vertebrae.

Gluteus Maximus: This is the large muscle located at the top of the legs, in the buttocks.

Quadriceps: The quadriceps are made up of four muscles located in the front of the thigh.

Hamstrings: The hamstrings are made up of three muscles found in the back of the thigh. These muscles help the leg bend at the knee.

Adductors: The adductors muscles are located at the top of the thigh, just below the gluteus maximus. These muscles help to swing the legs in from the side and to bring them across the body.

Abductors: The abductors are located beneath the quadriceps. They help to swing the legs out from the body, moving at the hip.

Gastrocnemius: This is the calf muscle located at the back of the lower leg.

Gross anatomy: The study of visible anatomy. Sometimes it is referred to as topographic anatomy. The gross anatomy of the body is described either in terms of regions of the body or in terms of body parts. Gross anatomy can also be described according to the body's different systems, such as the skeletal-muscular system.

Functional anatomy: Studies how the body systems operate, how they interrelate to accomplish various functions, and the consequences of improper function.

Biomechanics: Studies how energy and force act upon or are created by the human body. For example, biomechanics is used to describe the forces and movements involved with a normal walking gait.

Glycolysis: Adenosine triphosphate (ATP) production can be done aerobically or anaerobically. One anaerobic method of production is called glycolysis. It involves the rapid breakdown of carbohydrates into pyruvate, which can produce ATP.

Heat Stress: When the core body temperature rises due to environment changes, metabolic changes, or improper clothing, it is known as heat stress.

Hemodynamics: During exertion, blood flow and composition undergo changes. This phenomenon is known as hemodynamics.

Hypoxic ventilatory response: When an individual is exposed to the lower air pressure and lower oxygen content of high altitudes, he may begin to breathe more rapidly in response. This is called the hypoxic ventilatory response.

Clavicle: The clavicle bone is located above the rib cage. It is commonly called the collarbone.

Scapula: The scapula are the bones in the back that connect with the shoulder. They are commonly called the shoulder blades.

Sternum: The sternum is located in the middle of the rib cage and runs vertically down the chest.

Humerus: The bone located in the upper arm.

Ulna and radius: The two bones located in the forearm. The ulna is the larger of the two. The radius is located on the same side of the arm as the thumb.

Femur: The bone located in the thigh.

Fibula and tibia: The two bones located in the lower leg. The tibia is larger and is also known as the shinbone.

Carpals and tarsals: The smaller bones located in the wrists and ankles. The carpals are in the wrists. The tarsals are in the ankles.

Review Video: Anatomy of Personal Training
Visit mometrix.com/academy and enter code: 229409

Normal physical responses

While warming up, the individual begins to move the body at a faster, but not strenuous rate. This increases blood flow to the muscles, gradually prepares the heart for greater exertion, and readies the nerve-to-muscle pathways to respond to greater activity. Cooling down should be done at the same pace as the warm-up, but after exertion. It helps circulation and respiration return to normal gradually, which can prevent dizziness. It also helps remove lactic acid from the muscles, which can reduce soreness.

During cardiovascular exercise, the cardiovascular and respiratory system work harder. The body needs more oxygen to support exertion, so breathing is faster. Greater blood flow is also necessary, so the heart beats at a higher rate. During strength training, the skeletal muscles act against some other force—weights and elastic cords, for example. When a muscle is challenged to lift more than it can, the body responds by building strength in that muscle over time.

Skinfold measurements

As the exercise specialist, you will need to be able to estimate a patient's body fat percentage. This will help you to assess overall health and set appropriate fitness goals. Body fat is usually estimated by taking skinfold measurements, using a set of special calipers. There are several places on the body where skinfold measures can be made: the diagonal fold along the chest; the vertical fold on the midaxillary; the diagonal fold just below the shoulder blades; the vertical fold along the back or front of the arm; the vertical fold of the abdomen just to the right of the belly button; the vertical fold along the back of the thigh; or the vertical fold along the side of the calf.

Body circumference measurements

Measurements of the circumference of various parts of the body can also be useful in assessing health and setting goals. To take these measurements, the exercise specialist uses a tape measure. Typically, seven measurements are made. The upper arm is measured where the bicep is thickest (usually midway between the elbow and shoulder). The forearm is measured at its thickest point as well. The abdomen is measured around the belly button. The waist measurement is taken at the narrowest point between the chest and hips. The hips are measured at the point of maximum circumference. The thigh and calf are also measured at the thickest points. These measurements help you to determine the patient's frame size and body mass index.

When taking body circumference measurements, it is important to follow a standard procedure in order to get consistent and accurate results. First, you should use a tension-regulated tape to make the measurements. Measurements of the arms and legs should be taken on the right side of the body. Have the patient stand while taking the measurements. Make sure the patient uses good posture, but also stays relaxed. The tape should wrap around the area being measured and be perpendicular to the long axis of the body or limb. Pull the tape taut, but do not cause the skin to pinch. Take each measurement twice. Start over if the two measurements differ by more than a quarter-inch.

Skeletal system

Axial and appendicular skeleton

The human skeleton can be divided into two parts for the convenience of easier study. The first is the axial skeleton. This refers to all the bones that make up the center axis of the body, including the skull, the spine, the ribs, and the sternum. The skull contains 29 bones, most of which move very little. The exception is the jawbone. The spine contains 33 vertebrae along with intervertebral disks. The ribs and sternum create a protective structure around the heart and lungs.

The appendicular skeleton includes the bones of the arms, legs, pectoral girdle, and pelvic girdle. The clavicles (collar bones) at the top of the sternum and the scapulae (shoulder blades) are included in the appendicular skelcton.

Bones

The bones make up the supportive structure of the body. The bones connect at the joints—the points of movement such as the knee, ankle, shoulder, or wrist. The success of an exercise movement depends on the easy coordinated movement of the bones. If there are issues with the bones or joints, the exercise specialist must consider the issues when forming an exercise plan. While the bones provide the supporting structure for the body, the muscles make actual movement possible. By expanding and contracting, the muscles move the body in myriad ways. The bones and muscles are attached with two kinds of connective tissues: tendons and ligaments. Muscles are connected to bones via tendons. When a muscle contracts, the tendon connection between the muscle and bone allows for bone movement to occur. (Inflamed tendons are a common injury.) Ligaments connect bones to each other at the joints and help form the supportive structure of the skeleton. Ligaments are not as elastic as tendons.

Bones are made up of calcium and other minerals. They are wrapped in a protective sheath that separates them from other tissues and connects them to the body's circulatory system. Compact bone is dense, while cancellous bone is spongy.

The bones are the foundation of the body's structure. Without bones, movement as we know it would be impossible. The bones also help to protect the internal organs , and work with the muscles to enable movement. Bones are also where blood cells are generated.

The four types of bones are long bones, short bones, flat bones and irregular bones. Long bones are found in the arms and legs, short bones are found in places like the wrists and ankles, flat bones are found in the skull and ribs, and irregular bones are those like the vertebrae.

Muscular system

Brain controls muscle movements

The muscle fibers are controlled by motor neurons, which are part of the central nervous systems. Together the motor neuron and all the muscles to which it provides signals make up a motor unit. Different motor units are signaled separately for each muscle contraction. The motor neuron signals its muscles fibers through the neuro-muscular junction. Each motor neuron has a synaptic knob containing acetylcholine. Acetylcholine is a neurotransmitter. The sarcolemma, on the muscle-end of the process has receptors that receive acetylcholine. When movement is desired, the brain signals the muscle through the central nervous system. The motor neuron receives the signal, which triggers a reaction along the neuro-muscular junction. Acetylcholine is released into the sarcolemma, where it causes the muscle to contract.

Muscle cells

Muscle cells are complex structures. The part of the cell surrounding the nucleus is called sarcoplasm. From the sarcolemma, there are tubules that reach into the sarcoplasm. Their job is to relay signals to the sarcoplasmic reticulum, where calcium is stored. The cells also contain myofibrils, which have myofilaments within them. The myofilaments are made up of actin and myosin, the proteins responsible for muscle contractions. Another element is tropomyosin, which is necessary for muscle relaxation. Together all of these components make it possible for muscles to contract and relax.

Muscles in exercise

Movements occur in three planes described in relation to the body. The planes are the frontal plane, the transverse plane, and the sagittal plane. The frontal plane divides the body vertically down the middle, separating front and back. The sagittal plane runs vertical and perpendicular to the frontal plane, dividing the body into left and right sections. The transverse plane runs horizontally and divides the upper half of the body from the lower half.

Each muscle action occurs in one or more planes. For example, movements of the hips can occur in any of the three planes. Flexing the hip to the side is a sagittal motion, rolling the pelvis upward is a frontal motion, and rotating the hips in a circle is a transverse motion. Movements of the knee, on the other hand, happen only in the sagittal plane.

Myotatic stretch reflex

Muscle fibers contain muscle spindle. During stretching, the muscle spindle reacts to changes in the muscle length and the speed with which the changes occur. The myotatic stretch reflex occurs in response to the changes. It is a resistance force, causing the muscles to contract against the stretch. The reflex occurs in direct proportion to the timing of the stretch. Fast lengthening leads to a fast contraction. The myotatic stretch reflex helps prevent injuries that might occur from rapid alterations in the length of a muscle.

Temporarily overcoming the myotatic reflex is important in increasing flexibility. This is the reason for holding stretches. As a person holds a muscle in a lengthened state, the muscle spindle adjusts to the new length and stops the reflex.

Respiratory muscles

The respiratory muscles are part of the skeletal-muscular system. The muscles make inhalation and exhalation possible. The muscles that work during inhalation include the diaphragm, the external intercostal muscles, and the parasternal muscles. For exhalation, the muscles involved include the internal intercostal muscles and the abdominal muscles.

The intercostal muscles and the parasternal muscles are all located between the ribs. The diaphragm is located just below the sternum and the abdominal muscles are located in the abdomen.

At rest, the muscles described for exhalation aren't actually required. At rest, exhalation is passive. However during exertion, the muscles work to expel air more quickly.

Cardiovascular system

Heart

The heart is made up of four chambers. The two chambers at the top are known as the right and left atria. The two chambers at the bottom are the left and right ventricles. There is a membrane separating the atria from the ventricles. It is called the coronary sulcus. The muscle walls surrounding the atria are much thinner than those surrounding the ventricles. Oxygenated blood from the lungs enters the heart through the left pulmonary vein into the left atrium. It travels through the bicuspid valve into the left ventricle then through the aortic semilunar valve into the ascending aorta, where it goes into the general circulatory system. Blood in need of oxygen enters the right atrium, passes through the tricuspid valve into the right ventricle, and then moves into the pulmonic semilunar valve. From there it enters the pulmonary arteries where it travels to the lungs.

Arteries, capillaries, and veins

The arteries carry blood away from the heart. They are lined with muscle cells. As they get farther from the heart, the arteries become smaller and smaller. Small arteries are called arterioles. The arterioles connect to capillaries. The capillaries are small vessels that deliver nutrients in the blood to the cells and tissues. The capillaries also collect waste products from the cells and tissues and move them into veins where they are carried away to be removed, either through the elimination system or the respiratory system. Veins take blood toward the heart. The blood will travel through the lungs where it will become oxygenated again. Then the blood will move to the heart, where it will be pumped out through the arteries, starting the process over again.

Respiratory system

The respiratory system is divided into the upper respiratory tract and the lower respiratory tract. The upper tract includes the nose, the sinuses, the pharynx, and the larynx. The trachea and the lungs make up the lower tract. Within the lungs are the bronchi, bronchioles, and the alveoli. Each person has two lungs. The right lung is larger and has three separate lobes. The left lung has only two. When a person breathes in, air passes through the sinuses where it is heated, moistened, and cleaned. The air then travels through the pharynx and the larynx into the trachea. The trachea allows the air to pass into the lungs, at which point it travels through the bronchial system to the alveoli, where the oxygen can enter the blood. When a person exhales, the process is reversed and carbon dioxide is removed from the body.

C-shaped cartilage rings

There are several C-shaped cartilage "rings" within the trachea. They are open on one side, making them C-shaped rather than truly ring-shaped. These cartilage structures play a number of important roles. First, they provide a semi-rigid structure that supports the trachea and keeps the trachea's opening clear. Otherwise, the trachea might collapse and obstruct the airway. The cartilage also provides a counterforce to changes in respiratory pressure. This keeps the trachea from over-expanding, which could cause an injury. The C-shaped cartilages are positioned so that the open end of the C is in front of the esophagus, which allows swallowing to happen without impeding the airway.

Cardiovascular and respiratory cooperation

The cardiovascular and respiratory systems work together to carry oxygen and other vital nutrients to the cells throughout the body. The heart is the center of the cardiovascular system. By expanding and contracting regularly, the heart pumps blood through a system of arteries and veins so that the blood can reach all the cells of the body. The lungs are the center of the respiratory system. Blood passes from the heart and goes through the lungs, where it becomes oxygenated. Then, through the continued action of the heart, the blood carries the oxygen throughout the body, nourishing cells and tissues.

Cardiovascular and respiratory cooperation

The cardiovascular and respiratory systems work together to carry oxygen and other vital nutrients to the cells throughout the body. The heart is the center of the cardiovascular system. By expanding and contracting regularly, the heart pumps blood through a system of arteries and veins so that the blood can reach all the cells of the body. The lungs are the center of the respiratory system. Blood passes from the heart and goes through the lungs, where it becomes oxygenated. Then, through the continued action of the heart, the blood carries the oxygen throughout the body, nourishing cells and tissues.

Acute cardiorespiratory responses

During exercise, the body requires more oxygen. In response, changes occur in the heart rate, stroke volume, cardiac output, blood flow, blood pressure, arteriovenous oxygen difference, and pulmonary ventilation.

The heart rate rises steadily with exertion. The beats occur more rapidly, shortening the time that the heart has to fill. The stroke volume is the amount of blood that comes out of the heart during each beat. During exercise, the stroke volume increases as the work rate increases. It plateaus when the body reaches about 50% of maximum exercise capacity.

Cardiac output is determined by the heart rate multiplied by the stroke volume. Naturally, it rises during exercise. During exercise, blood flow to the working muscles increases dramatically. Blood pressure rises. The arteriovenous oxygen difference (the difference in oxygen content of the blood in the arteries versus the veins) increases, as the blood in the veins has a lower oxygen content during exercise when the tissues demand more. Pulmonary ventilation—the breathing rate—also rises during exercise.

Factors

There are several factors that can affect acute cardiorespiratory responses. One factor is the position in which exercise takes place. At rest, stroke volume tends to be higher when an individual is lying down as opposed to when he is standing up. Stroke volume during an exercise in a supine position does not change much because of this fact, whereas stroke volume increases noticeably duri exercise performed standing up.

The type of exercise has an effect on acute responses. While cardiorespiratory responses are typical during dynamic exercise, there are few cardiorespiratory changes that occur during isometric exercise.

Because the legs have much larger muscles than the arms, exertion involving the legs causes bigger cardiorespiratory changes than exercise involving just the arms.

Lactic acid

Lactic acid is produced in the muscles in a variety of ways. When lactic acid levels in the blood begin to rise, muscle fatigue may be the result. For a long time, medical scientists thought that elevated lactic acid levels were a sign that a person was exceeding her aerobic capacity. The reasoning was that lactate is an end product of glycolysis when there is not enough oxygen present in the system.

Current theories hold that lactate is also produced when glycolysis occurs very rapidly, and fast-twitch muscles involved in exertion produce lactate more rapidly that slow-twitch muscles. It is likely that lactic acid levels are due to a combination of these factors.

Skeletal system

Axial and appendicular skeleton

The human skeleton can be divided into two parts for the convenience of easier study. The first is the axial skeleton. This refers to all the bones that make up the center axis of the body, including the skull, the spine, the ribs, and the sternum. The skull contains 29 bones, most of which move very little. The exception is the jawbone. The spine contains 33 vertebrae along with intervertebral disks. The ribs and sternum create a protective structure around the heart and lungs.

The appendicular skeleton includes the bones of the arms, legs, pectoral girdle, and pelvic girdle. The clavicles (collar bones) at the top of the sternum and the scapulae (shoulder blades) are included in the appendicular skeleton.

Bones

The bones make up the supportive structure of the body. The bones connect at the joints—the points of movement such as the knee, ankle, shoulder, or wrist. The success of an exercise movement depends on the easy coordinated movement of the bones. If there are issues with the bones or joints, the exercise specialist must consider the issues when forming an exercise plan. While the bones provide the supporting structure for the body, the muscles make actual movement possible. By expanding and contracting, the muscles move the body in myriad ways. The bones and muscles are attached with two kinds of connective tissues: tendons and ligaments. Muscles are connected to bones via tendons. When a muscle contracts, the tendon connection between the muscle and bone allows for bone movement to occur. (Inflamed tendons are a common injury.) Ligaments connect bones to each other at the joints and help form the supportive structure of the skeleton. Ligaments are not as elastic as tendons.

Bones are made up of calcium and other minerals. They are wrapped in a protective sheath that separates them from other tissues and connects them to the body's circulatory system. Compact bone is dense, while cancellous bone is spongy.

The bones are the foundation of the body's structure. Without bones, movement as we know it would be impossible. The bones also help to protect the internal organs , and work with the muscles to enable movement. Bones are also where blood cells are generated.

The four types of bones are long bones, short bones, flat bones and irregular bones. Long bones are found in the arms and legs, short bones are found in places like the wrists and ankles, flat bones are found in the skull and ribs, and irregular bones are those like the vertebrae.

Joints

The three categories of joints found in the body are fibrous, cartilaginous, and synovial. Fibrous joints include suture joints, syndesmosis joints, and gomphosis joints. Suture joints fit together tightly and occur only between the bones of the skull. Syndesmosis joints occur between the two long bones in the forearm and in the calf. Gomphosis joints are those that occur between a tooth and its socket. Cartilaginous joints come in two types—primary and secondary. Primary cartilaginous joints usually allow bones to grow and fuse. Exceptions include the sternum and the costal cartilage between ribs. Secondary joints are strong and able to move but only a little. One example of synovial joints is the joints between intervertebral discs. Synovial joints make up the majority of the joints and allow for most of the movements between bones in the body. The types of synovial joints are gliding, hinge, condyloid, saddle, ball and socket, and pivot.

Synovial joints

The synovial joints are those that provide the body with most of its ability to move. These joints are found at the intersection of two or more bones. The joints are covered with cartilage and lined with synovial membranes.

The primary types are ball-and-socket, condyloid, gliding, hinge, pivot, and saddle. The shoulder joint is a ball-and-socket joint. It allows for full rotation and angular movements in every plane. The wrist is an example of a condyloid joint. It allows for rotation, as well as flexion and extension movements. The ankle is an example of a gliding joint, the knee is an example of a hinge joint, the atlas joint (at the hips) is a pivot joint, and the thumb is a saddle joint.

Connective tissue in skeletal muscles

Skeletal muscles are made up of three layers of connective tissue. They are the epimysium, perimysium, and endomysium. The innermost layer is the endomysium. Each individual muscle fiber has a surrounding layer of endomysium. Each muscle is divided into compartments of muscle fibers. The perimysium divides the compartments. Each muscle is also wrapped in a layer of tissues that separates it from other tissues and from organs. This layer is the epimysium. The epimysium also forms the tendon at the end of the muscle, which connects the muscle to the bone.

Physical Activity and Health Promotion

Healthy lifestyle

The personal trainer is very instrumental in helping the client understand what options are available for a healthy lifestyle. The personal trainer can take time at each session to discuss with the client the choices he has made throughout the week and how he can be more effective by choosing healthier options. The personal trainer becomes a mentor, source of accountability, cheerleader, and coach for the client and must encourage honest communication so the client can receive the best results of his programming.

Lifestyle management techniques and health coaching principles

One example of a lifestyle management technique is to have the client keep a food log and an activity log each week. The trainer can take the logs, make suggestions, and return the logs to the client to help promote change. Another example is to help the client identify sources of stress in her life and help create alternatives for managing it. Anytime the client can help in creating solutions to issues that stand in the way of well-being and health, the more likely she will be to follow through on the course of action.

Reducing risk

Physical activity is an effective way to reduce the risk of a number of chronic diseases and diseases associated with aging. An analysis of studies comparing individuals who work in physically active jobs with those who don't found that the non-active individuals had a 40% higher risk of heart disease. Recreational activity is even more important. Individuals who are not active outside of work have a 90% greater risk of heart disease. A sedentary lifestyle increases the risk of stroke up to three times compared to an active lifestyle. Inactivity raises hypertension risks between 30 and 40 percent when compared to an active lifestyle. It raises the risks of type 2 diabetes by up to 60% compared with an active lifestyle. Physical activity also significantly reduces the risks of many kinds of cancer.

Wellness

Wellness is a lifestyle model that includes a person's bodily, religious, and psychological health. It can be perceived as a means to prevention of disease by performing actions that reduce a person's likelihood of developing certain conditions. In addition, wellness is a goal for the best possible health and functioning of the whole person.

Wellness is often mistaken for only a healthy diet and exercise routine, but it is more than that. It is an ongoing lifestyle, not an achievable or static state of being. Wellness can be expressed as a continuum ranging from death to optimal health and satisfaction in life.

Influence of lifestyle factors on lipid and lipoprotein levels

A sedentary lifestyle, poor nutrition, and high stress levels are the most influential factors that cause unhealthy lipid levels for clients. When clients begin a normal exercise routine, begin to make healthy food choices, and learn to manage their stress more effectively, they notice a difference in their lipid levels. Genetics can play a role in predisposing a client to have high lipid profiles, but it takes unhealthy lifestyle choices to cause their genes to create poor health.

Screening, Evaluation, and Professional Practice

Pre-screening process

During the pre-screening process, the personal trainer follows a series of steps to ensure the comfort of the patient and to ensure that nothing important is missed. The first step is to ask for the patient's express consent for the pre-screening. After receiving the patient's consent, the personal trainer takes a formal medical history for the patient. Often this step will reveal a number of potential risk factors or important points for the personal trainer to consider. The third step is to discuss exercise goals with the patient. This step is crucial for a successful program. Next, the personal trainer identifies the patient's risk factors. If an exercise test is appropriate, the personal trainer will recommend the test best suited to the patient's needs. The personal trainer has to decide if his or her facility can handle the testing or if the patient should be referred to another facility. The results of the exercise test help the specialist determine the best exercise program for the patient's health needs and fitness goals.

Review Video: 4 Skills Every Personal Trainer Should Have
Visit mometrix.com/academy and enter code: 588982

Medical background

The fundamental goal of the personal trainer during pre-screening is to determine if a patient can safely begin an exercise program. During the course of pre-screening, the personal trainer may need to determine whether or not exercise testing is needed. The personal trainer will also recommend whether or not the patient needs medical supervision when beginning an exercise program, and if so, what degree of supervision is prudent. In the process of pre-screening, the personal trainer will identify what contraindications the patient has, if there are factors that put the patient at increased risk, and if the patient has any special needs. All this information will be used to design an exercise program appropriate for the patient.

During the medical history, the personal trainer need to determine past or current events or conditions that may affect the patient's ability to exercise safely. Some of the things the personal trainer should ask about include diagnoses of chronic diseases or diseases with lasting effects, any hospitalizations or surgeries the patient has experienced, any medications that the patient is taking, and any family history of illness. The personal trainer should also ask about current activities that the patient engages in. It may be that the patient has recently undergone exercise testing. If so, the results of the test will be relevant to the evaluation. The specialist should also determine any existing symptoms that the patient is contending with and how frequent and severe the symptoms are.

Risk factors

Risk factors, otherwise known as positive risk factors, are circumstances that increase the patient's risk of a condition or disease. A negative risk factor is one that provides protection against a condition or disease, lowering the patient's risk. Some of the risk factors the personal trainer should account for during the pre-screening process are the following: family history of disease; history of smoking or current smoking habit; high blood pressure; high cholesterol levels; high fasting glucose levels; obesity; and sedentary lifestyle. Negative risk factors include high levels of HDL cholesterol, an active lifestyle, and healthy eating habits.

Symptoms

The personal trainer is primarily concerned with symptoms that occur when the patient exerts himself or attempts to exercise. The most common symptoms that the personal trainer should take note of are pain or discomfort in the area of the chest; shortness of breath; high levels of fatigue triggered by physical activity; dizziness; heart palpitations or a confirmed heart murmur; pain in the legs; and breathing irregularities. Each of these symptoms can help to indicate to the specialist what problems the patient may encounter when exercising and how to develop a safe exercise program that will assist the patient in improving his or her condition.

Physical factors

During the pre-screening process, the personal trainer screens physical factors as well as taking a medical history. As a personal trainer, you need to take a patient's blood pressure both when she is lying down on her back and when she is standing up. You also want to measure the patient's heart rate and blood pressure after mild exertion such as walking to the end of the hall and back. You should listen to the patient's heartbeat, checking for any abnormalities not listed in the patient's history. You should listen to the patient's lungs, as well. You will also take the patient's pulse and examine her musculoskeletal system for any abnormalities.

Lab tests

There are several lab tests that a personal trainer might perform during a medical pre-screening. Among these are a complete blood count (CBC), a urinary analysis, a measure of blood glucose, a measure of creatine levels, and a measure of cholesterol levels. Each of these tests can indicate medical conditions that might determine the type of exercise program appropriate for the patient. For example, a CBC might uncover that the patient has anemia—low iron levels in the blood. Anemia can cause the patient to fatigue quickly, which would make strenuous exercise difficult. In this case you would need to address the anemia as well as tailor exercise recommendations appropriately. In some cases, EKG testing and other stress level testing also may be appropriate.

Contraindications

In some cases, exercise testing may present a danger to the patient. The personal trainer must recognize the contraindications that absolutely rule out exercise testing. Those contraindications include a recent heart attack or myocardial infarction, unstable angina, an uncontrolled arrhythmia, aortic stenosis with severe symptoms, uncontrolled heart failure, pulmonary embolus, the presence of a dissecting aneurysm, or the existence of an acute infection. In addition, some conditions require caution when testing, but testing may still be beneficial. (In these cases, the personal trainer or supervising physician must determine if the risks outweigh the benefits.) These include moderate arrhythmias, moderate cardiopulmonary conditions, metabolic disorders, bone disorders, or chronic infections. The personal trainer should also look for electrolyte imbalances, hypertension, or conditions that impair mobility.

Medical background

The kinetic chain's function is altered by any type of injury or surgery. To determine which activities may be contraindicated for certain dysfunctions, the CPT must ask clients about their medical histories.

Be sure to ask about:

- Injuries and/or pain, including:
    - Sprains of the ankle, groin, or hamstrings;

    - Tendinitis of the shoulders, knee (patellar), shins (posterior tibialis), or arch of the foot (plantar fasciitis);
    - Chronic headaches.
- Surgeries, especially those that:
    - Are performed on the joints (shoulder, back, knee, ankle, or foot);
    - Involve cutting of the abdominal wall (Cesarean section or appendectomy).
- Chronic conditions or diseases, such as:
    - Coronary heart/artery disease or congestive heart failure;
    - Cardiovascular disease or hypertension;
    - High cholesterol;
    - Lung or breathing problems;
    - Diabetes mellitus.
- Any medications.

PAR-Q

PAR-Q stands for Physical Activity Readiness Questionnaire. The first step in finding out a client's general history, this yes-or-no test is intended to determine whether a person has a cardiorespiratory dysfunction (such as coronary heart disease). It not only alerts the CPT to clients who may need medical attention but it also allows the health and fitness professional to assign clients appropriate activity levels: from low to medium to high.

Questions on the PAR-Q are intended to determine whether a potential client:

- Feels chest pain (at any time);
- Loses balance or consciousness;
- Experiences bone or joint problems;
- Takes medication for high blood pressure or a heart condition;
- Knows of any other reason that he or she should not perform physical activity.

Medical risk factors

Evidence supports the hypothesis that muscular and skeletal ailments are more prevalent in modern society than they were a generation ago. Many factors contribute to this decline in the health of the average American. An increase in automation and a decrease in physical activity have altered the overall health and physical fitness level of Americans over the last century. A good deal of research has been done on subjects such as:

- Low back pain—This problem is estimated to affect four out of five American adults and is common among those who work in offices and remain seated for long periods of time.
- Knee injuries—There are approximately 100,000 injuries to the anterior cruciate ligament (ACL) each year, with the vast majority resulting from non-sport-related incidents. Most of these injuries occur to young people between the ages of 15 and 25 and may be a result of a less-active population.
- Chronic disease—A decrease in activity can lead to or exacerbate chronic problems such as obesity, diabetes, hypertension, and other heart conditions.
- Kinetic chain injuries—In recent years, these types of injuries ranked near the top reasons for visits to the doctor. These are often caused by poor posture resulting from repetitive sitting and lack of muscle support caused by sedentary lifestyles.

Important assessments

Heart rate recovery

During exercise the heart rate goes up. After exercise the heart rate returns to normal. This is called recovery. This process of increased heart rate and recovery is part of the body's vagal activity. A reduction in vagal activity is a sign of increased risk of death from cardiovascular problems.

When doing exercising testing, the personal trainer should measure the recovery heart rate. To do this, note the heart rate during peak performance and then note the heart rate again one minute after exercise is complete. The heart should fall by more than 12 beats per minute (bpm) in that time. If it does not, it is a sign of decreased vagal activity, which increases relative risk of death by up to four times. A slow recovery should be noted by the personal trainer and considered when devising a safe exercise plan for the patient.

Target heart rate

Part of the exercise assessment process involves finding a patient's target heart rate. The target heart rate is a guideline the patient can use to make sure that they are working out at a proper intensity—one that is neither too strenuous nor too easy.

A patient's maximum heart rate is generally considered to be 220 minus the patient's age. The target heart rate is a range of 50 to 85 percent of maximum. Depending on the patient's fitness level and resting heart rate, the personal trainer may need to adjust the maximum and target heart rate in order to ensure the patient's safety and success.

Blood pressure

Blood pressure is a strong indicator of cardiovascular health and risks. If blood pressure is too high or too low, it may indicate that the patient has a serious health problem. Blood pressure that is too high also increases a patient's risk of experiencing a cardiac event during exercise. Blood pressure that is too low puts the patient at risk for dizzy spells, fainting and falls that could result in an injury. If a patient's blood pressure is below 80/60 or above 175/100, then the personal trainer should refer the patient to a physician before proceeding further. Recommending an exercise program to a patient outside of the safe range of blood pressures without the express consent of a physician could result in injury or death for the patient.

Fasting blood glucose

Elevated fasting blood glucose can indicate a metabolic disorder or diabetes. Both can mean that patient is at higher risk of heart disease. The personal trainer may need to adjust the exercise program to accommodate these factors, or may need to consult with the patient's physician.

When interpreting the fasting blood glucose levels, you must know what is normal, what is worrisome, and what is obviously too high. The normal range of fasting blood glucose is 60 to 109 mg per deciliter (mg/dL) of blood. A blood glucose level between 110 and 125 mg/dL is a sign of impaired glucose function. The patient may not be aware that they are at risk of diabetes—a doctor visit is important. If blood glucose is 126 mg/dL or above, the patient has diabetes.

Body composition

The measuring of body composition by air displacement, also known as a BOD POD measurement, takes place in a chamber built for the purpose. The chamber consists of two sections, one for the subject and one for instrumentation. There is a flexible section of material in the wall between the two sections. The volume and pressure of the air in the subject section are measured while it is empty, and then again after the subject enters. Pressure and volume before and after are used to estimate body fat, body volume and body density.

Hydrostatic weighing refers to weighing an individual underwater. Because body fat is buoyant and other body mass is not, underwater weight provides a method to calculate body density and body fat.

Bioelectrical impedance uses a low-level electrical current run through the body. The resistance is measured and used to calculate body density and body fat. This is the simplest of the procedures and requires the least complicated equipment.

<u>Subjective and objective measurements</u>

- Objective Measurements: Objective measurements or objective methods are ways of evaluating exercise that are not swayed by personal input or perceptions. The accelerometer, heart rate monitor, and the pedometer all provide objective measures of physical activity.
- Subjective Measurements: These are measures or methods that require input either from the patient or the specialist. With subjective measures, a greater degree of interpretation is required by the personal trainer. An example of a subjective measure is a workout diary kept by the patient.

Both subjective and objective measures are important when evaluating a patient. Together the two can provide you with a good understanding of the patient's abilities, attitude, and commitment, as well as areas that are problematic for the patient.

Studies conducted on the effects of physical activity on risks of different diseases rely on either subjective or objective gathering of data. Each method has advantages and disadvantages.

Subjective data can be inaccurate because of faulty recall—people forget the time they have spent being active or overestimate their levels of activity. Often subjective methods are not comprehensive. Questions focus on certain kinds of activity and not others. The advantages of subjective methods are that they are not costly and they are usually easy to use. This makes it possible to gather data from a large group of individuals.

Objective methods are also not usually comprehensive. Participants may use monitors for some activities, but forget to use them for others. The results can also be skewed by unpredictable variables. Often objective methods are more expensive as well. The advantages are that objective methods are more accurate than subjective methods and are less obtrusive.

When choosing the best way to assess an individual patient, it's a good idea to look at a number of factors. First consider your purpose. Do you want to know more about the patient's activity levels over the past year or are you more interested in the patient's activity levels going forward? A questionnaire is better suited to an assessment of past activity, but a diary may be more appropriate as an ongoing assessment. How much time to you have to assess the data? You will likely get more data from a diary, which will require a greater commitment for analysis. How motivated is your patient? A diary will not work if the patient does not commit to making entries. The patient's age is also a factor. Very old or very young patients may do better with a questionnaire than a diary.

The two most common subjective methods of assessment are diaries and questionnaires. A diary is a daily recording made by a patient of her physical activity. A questionnaire involves the patient answering a series of questions provided by the personal trainer.

A diary does not require an interviewer or observer and can be maintained by the patient and reviewed periodically by the personal trainer. It can be more time consuming than a questionnaire because it may contain quite a lot of extra, irrelevant information. A diary also requires a higher level of commitment from the patient.

A questionnaire is sometimes an easier way to gather information from a patient. The personal trainer can make sure it is focused and targeted. However, a questionnaire may not be as accurate as a diary as the personal trainer needs the patient to recall activity levels over period of time instead of recording them as they happen.

Body mass index

The body mass index (BMI) accounts for a patient's height and proportions rather than focusing strictly on his weight. The standard body mass index is appropriate for adults, but not for children. (For children and teens, use an index tailored to their age.)

The BMI is calculated by taking the patient's weight in kilograms and dividing it by his height in meters. For example:

> If weight is 69 kg and height is 1.68 m (168 cm), then the BMI is $68/(1.68)^2$. This would equal 24.45.

If you are working in pounds and inches, divide the patient's weight in pounds by his height in inches and multiply that result by 703.

> For example, if weight is 148 lbs and height is 65 inches (5 foot, 5 inches), the BMI is $[148/(65)^2] \times 703$. The final BMI is 24.63.

Supervision for individuals who received medical clearance

Clients who have received medical clearance for exercise should be monitored continually during the exercise session. Additionally, they need to indicate how hard they feel they are working according to the RPE scale. These clients should never be left alone to exercise until they have come to a point where their risk factors are decreasing or it is deemed that they can exercise safely by themselves.

Continuing education

A personal trainer should keep abreast of changes and modifications within the field by attending regular continuing education. This can be done through taking classes that help to maintain certification or by receiving a degree in higher education. Training can be hands on, online, or in a classroom setting. The important thing is for the trainer to consider how this education will benefit her knowledge so that clients can ultimately benefit from it. The trainer should take classes that directly relate to the populations that she trains.

Scope of practice for certified personal trainers

The scope of practice for a personal trainer includes improving health and physical fitness as a means to prevent disease, health problems related to obesity, and premature aging. Personal trainers should not diagnose injuries or medical problems and should not attempt to perform the role of a physical therapist, athletic trainer, registered dietitian, or rehabilitation specialist. Although the trainer may understand certain concepts from other allied fitness professional fields, he is not licensed to practice them.

If a personal trainer practices outside the acceptable scope of practice, it can lead to negligence and false practice of other professions. A client may become injured when a personal trainer attempts to teach things she is not licensed to practice. Doing this increases the personal trainer's liability, and ultimately the client could sue for any damages that are a result of false practice. A personal trainer could potentially lose her business in such a situation.

Effective communication with allied professionals

If a client requires medical clearance to participate in a workout program, or has been referred to a personal trainer by a medical professional, it is appropriate to regularly communicate about the client's progress. The ideal ways for this to happen are through phone calls or postal service. Sensitive information should never be given through email or left on an answering machine, in order to protect patient privacy. The client also needs to be fully aware that information is being shared, and in the appropriate instances, sign a release of information.

Effective relationships with individuals in the greater health community

The personal trainer should always be aware that there are many different people invested in seeing a community grow in health and wellness. It would be to the personal trainer's benefit to network with like-minded medical and allied health professionals in the community by attending professional events and creating a strong referral system for clients to seek additional help that is outside the personal trainer's scope of practice. The trainer can partner with other professionals to provide special package pricing that includes multiple sessions of personal training combined with other professional services. Being active in the community and attending community health events is the best way for personal trainers to network with other health practitioners to reach a common goal.

Recommending other health services

When a personal trainer realizes that a client needs help in areas outside the trainer's scope of practice, the client needs to be referred. For instance, if a client needs more detailed information to help him nutritionally than is provided by the general guidelines found on www.myplate.gov, the client should be referred to a dietitian. If a client struggles excessively with finding solutions to stress management, and general guidelines for relaxation do not seem to suffice, the client should be referred to a life coach for further guidance.

CPR and AED

A personal trainer should maintain a current CPR/AED certification at all times. If a client becomes unconscious or stops breathing at any time, CPR protocol should be initiated. AED protocol should be initiated as necessary if there is more than one person at hand in a situation where a client collapses. If a personal trainer does not maintain a current CPR/AED certification, she could be held liable for practicing without a license.

Emergency procedures clearly delineated for the client

The personal trainer should make clear to the client proper procedure in case of emergencies. For instance, in case of a fire or inclement weather, the client should know where the exits are or where to seek adequate shelter. Whenever the fitness facility updates its procedures, it is the personal trainer's responsibility to ensure the client knows what to do. Additionally, the personal trainer should have on file permission from the client to call emergency services or a medical practitioner if appropriate.

Basic first-aid procedures

Exercise intolerance

If a client is experiencing exercise intolerance, a cooldown should be initiated immediately to bring the client's heart rate back down to resting levels. The client needs to drink adequate amounts of water to maintain hydration. The client should continue moving as necessary until heart rate returns to normal. If the client feels dizzy or overheated, he can sit down, but lying down is contraindicated. The client should be given some cool water, and a cold towel or compress should be applied to his neck to reduce body temperature. If the client is having trouble breathing due to chest pains, medical personnel should be contacted as it may be exercise-induced angina.

Exercise-related injury

If the client has an exercise-related injury, the client should be put in a sitting position and RICE (rest, ice, compression, elevation) should be followed for the injured area as needed. A medical practitioner should be immediately called. This information should be kept on file prior to any exercise sessions taking place so it can be accessed in the event of an emergency. The personal trainer should also have on file a client's permission to call emergency services in the event of an emergency if it's deemed necessary.

Client safety in the fitness facility

Client safety can be ensured by having them engage in exercises that correspond to their current fitness level. Clients should also be taught how to correctly handle resistance machines and free weights to avoid personal injury. They should also be made aware of facility rules regarding flow of traffic inside the facility, appropriate cardiovascular machine usage, and age requirements for using equipment. Clients should never use a machine they do not know how to use; this can be remedied by the personal trainer giving a comprehensive education on machine usage.

Nutrition and Weight Management

Carbohydrates—simple and complex

Carbohydrates are nutrients found in food that are the most common source of fuel for the body. After digesting carbohydrates, the body uses the resulting glucose for the brain. Additionally, carbohydrates are required for the body to break down stored fat. Carbohydrates are prominent in foods such as grains, sugars, fruits, and vegetables, as well as many refined or manufactured foods like sodas, candy, breads and pastries. Highly refined carbohydrates usually are devoid of fiber, vitamins, minerals and other micronutrients and should be eaten in very small amounts. Carbohydrates are especially important for athletes who participate in endurance sports. Carbohydrates have 4 calories per gram. Simple carbohydrates are those that are in an easy to process form, like sugar. Examples include sugars in candy, fruits, vegetables, and dairy products. Complex carbohydrates are usually combined with fiber and include foods such as breads, beans, and vegetables like potatoes and broccoli.

Protein—how it affects the body

Protein is a nutrient found in food that builds tissues in the body and makes hormones. Twenty-two different amino acids are necessary to make protein, and the human body only makes 13 of those, so the rest are required to be taken in as food. These 9 amino acids are considered essential amino acids. Complete proteins include all of the necessary amino acids and come from animal-based foods, such as meats. Incomplete proteins do not include all of the necessary amino acids for making proteins and are usually plant-based, such as beans or nuts. Protein has 4 calories per gram. Too much protein can cause kidney damage and elimination of calcium from the body. Athletes may need more protein because it is used as an energy source during long bouts of exercise and is needed to rebuild muscles that are worked and/or damaged.

Fats—different types; how they are used by the body

Fat is a nutrient found in food that is necessary for energy generation; keeping the organs, skin and hair healthy; moving fat-soluble vitamins through the body; and increases the risk of many diseases when ingested in high quantities. Fat has 9 calories per gram.

Triglycerides are the primary kind of fat found in food and in the body.

Saturated fats are usually from animal-based foods, but some oils are high in saturated fats. They increase the low-density lipoproteins (LDL) in the blood, thus increasing the risk of heart disease.

Unsaturated fats are:

- Monounsaturated fats lower the levels of LDL in the blood, which lowers the risk of heart disease.
- Polyunsaturated fats can reduce the risk of heart disease.

Trans fatty acids form when unsaturated fats are turned into semi-solids. They increase LDL levels and lower high density lipoproteins (HDL), greatly increasing the risk of heart disease.

Ways to lower amount of fat eaten

- Read nutrition labels on packaged food. Determine the percentage of calories that come from fat in the food. Everyone should aim to eat less than 30% of daily calories from fat.
- Eat more fish and chicken and less red meat.
- Eat less meat overall, and instead eat more vegetarian meals.
- Eat smaller amounts of food, and eat meats that are low in fat.
- When choosing fats, choose more unsaturated fats and fewer saturated and trans-fats. If buying a product that has saturated fats, make sure there is at least double the amount of unsaturated fats as saturated fats and has very little trans fats.
- Do not fry foods, but cook in lower fat ways.
- Eat fewer snack foods.

Cholesterol—definition; two types of lipoproteins

Cholesterol is a nutrient that is found in animal-based food, but is also made by the body. It is necessary for the body to make cells, hormones, and bile. However, too much cholesterol in the blood is a risk factor for atherosclerosis. Eating a diet high in fat is a direct cause of having excess cholesterol in the blood. Cholesterol is transported through the body by lipoproteins.

The ***two*** **types** are:

- ***High density lipoproteins (HDL)*** – considered "good" cholesterol, these lipoproteins help to clean the walls of the blood vessels and thus prevent atherosclerosis. A high level of HDL cholesterol lowers the risk of heart disease.
- ***Low density lipoproteins (LDL)*** – considered "bad" cholesterol, these lipoproteins help deposits to form on the walls of the blood vessels and thus increase the risk of atherosclerosis. A high level of LDL cholesterol is a risk factor for heart disease.

LDH vs. HDL

When too much LDL cholesterol circulates in the blood, it can slowly build up in the inner walls of the arteries that feed the heart and brain. Together with other substances it can form plaque, a thick, hard deposit that can clog those arteries. This condition is known as atherosclerosis. If a clot forms and blocks a narrowed artery, it can cause a heart attack or stroke. The levels of HDL cholesterol and LDL cholesterol in the blood are measured to evaluate the risk of having a heart attack. LDL cholesterol of less than 100 mg/dL is the optimal level. Less than 130 mg/dL is near optimal for most people. A high LDL level (more than 160 mg/dL or 130 mg/dL or above if you have two or more risk factors for cardiovascular disease) reflects an increased risk of heart disease.

About one-third to one-fourth of blood cholesterol is carried by high-density lipoprotein (HDL). HDL cholesterol is known as the "good" cholesterol because a high level of it seems to protect against heart attack. Medical experts think that HDL tends to carry cholesterol away from the arteries and back to the liver, where it's passed from the body. Some experts believe that HDL removes excess cholesterol from plaque in arteries, thus slowing the buildup.

Water—its role in the body; risks of dehydration; guidelines for water intake for athletes and anyone doing exercise

Water in blood helps move energy in the form of glucose to all areas of the body and take waste products away from the cells through the blood, and then in the urine. Water in sweat helps to cool the body. Anyone doing strenuous workouts should make sure to drink enough water to prevent dehydration, which is the lack of enough water in the body to continue the body's processes. Early signs of dehydration are headache, getting very tired and not doing as well at the activity. Ultimately, untreated dehydration can lead to cramps, fainting, or overheating (such as heat exhaustion or heat stroke).

Guidelines for water **intake** are

- Drink a half-liter of water two hours before each workout.
- Drink plenty of room temperature water during the workout.
- Someone doing endurance activities that last more than an hour should drink fluids that have added carbohydrates and electrolytes.

Nutrient density; glycemic index; glycemic load

- *Nutrient density* is the ratio of healthy nutrients in a food compared to the number of calories in that food. A very nutrient dense food will be low in calories and have at least 5% of the U.S. RDA of any of the recommended nutrients. Foods that are not nutrient dense will have high calories and few or no nutrients and are often called "junk" foods.
- *Glycemic Index* is a way to determine how carbohydrates affect the levels of glucose in the blood. This is based on how fast a food is digested, how much and what kind of fiber is present, how it is prepared, how ripe it is, and what other nutrients are present. The GI is based on 50 grams of the carbohydrate. *Glycemic Load* helps determine which foods will affect blood sugar the most, by multiplying the GI by the grams of carbohydrate in the food.

Designing a program of eating before and after strenuous exercise—carbohydrate loading and using the glycemic index (gi)

By eating the right amount of carbohydrates before a workout, the body will have energy to complete the activity without using the blood glucose too soon. Foods with low GI numbers release glucose into the blood slowly and over time, while foods that have high GI numbers release glucose into the blood in a short burst soon after eating. Low GI foods are better for eating before a workout, while high GI foods are good for eating after a workout.

Carbohydrate loading uses this principle to maximize the amount of energy stored in the cells for a strenuous workout. For 3 days before an athletic event, eat a diet composed of 60-70% carbohydrates. After a workout, eat 50 grams of a low-fat carbohydrate with a high GI number immediately after finishing, and then eat another 50 grams of a similar GI level food 2 hours later.

Fats and carbohydrates used for energy

When resting, the body uses about one calorie per minute, half from carbohydrates and half from fats. During lower intensity exercise, fats and carbohydrates are used equally. Fats can only be used for energy in the presence of oxygen, so as oxygen is depleted, anaerobic systems for energy must be utilized. As the body works harder, during higher intensity exercise, fewer fats and more carbohydrate is used. Keep in mind that while exercising at lower intensities burns a greater percentage of fat, people who are trying to lose weight must increase the total number of calories used, so working at a lower intensity will not necessarily accomplish this goal.

Energy balance—forces to consider

Energy balance means that staying at the same body weight requires that the calories taken in must be equal to the calories used. The resting metabolic rate (RMR) is the speed at which the body uses energy to maintain the processes of life (breathing, etc.). Most of the calories taken in are used for life processes. RMR is impacted by a person's age, gender, height, and activity level, but also the temperature of the air. RMR can be also be lowered if a person eats far too few calories. The activity level of a person (called the energy expended with exertion) includes the daily tasks a person does, any exercise performed, and the time immediately following exercise. The thermic effect of food is the rise in the metabolism when a person is digesting food. This is approximately 10% of the food's calorie count.

Suggestions trainers can give clients who want to lose weight

- Diet combined with exercise is the most effective weight loss strategy.
- Concentrate on changes that will increase health for life rather than short-term weight loss.
- Focus on using 500 more calories than are eaten each day.
- The person may lose momentum in the program, but that can be overcome.
- Beware of setting goals for the perfect weight.
- Even small amounts of weight loss can have enormous health benefits.
- Develop strategies for changing habits by changing shopping habits, food preparation, and restaurant choices, as well as avoiding situations where unhealthy eating is triggered.
- Instruct people about appropriate amounts of food.
- Have the person keep a log of everything she eats for a period of time in order to analyze the diet.
- Make a list of activities to do to prevent eating from being a reaction to boredom.
- It is ok to cheat occasionally, as long as the overall path is a healthy one.

The MyPyramid system—problems:

The MyPyramid system recommends that half of the carbohydrates eaten in a day be whole grains, so many people may assume that they should eat half of their carbohydrates as refined flour products, although these should be strictly limited. The protein recommendations equate low-fat, natural sources of protein with high-fat, manufactured proteins, even though natural, low-fat sources are the better choice. Many people disagree that the number of dairy servings that are recommended are either too low or too high. While the online MyPyramid system is sophisticated and customized for each user, the static diagram is unclear. In addition, the online standard prevents those who do not have a computer from using the system.

Ways in which supplement manufacturers may try to represent their products as valid performance enhancers

- The claims may be based on research with unsound designs that are not based on the scientific method.
- The package may state that studies are ongoing, which means that there is no evidence that the product works.
- The advertising may imply that the product is needed for a condition that is not necessarily a problem, nor is the product actually necessary.
- There may be testimonials or endorsements by reputable organization that did not actually endorse the product.
- The packaging may feature quotes from users of the product instead of featuring true facts about the scientific research.
- The packaging may feature a patent number and represent it as if the product was supported by the government.

- Ads for the product may be designed to look like news.
- The product may claim that more of a good thing is better.

Dietary references and nutrition labels

- DVs (Daily Values): a new dietary reference term that will appear on the food label. It is made up of two sets of references, DRVs and RDIs.
- DRVs (Daily Reference Values): a set of dietary references that applies to fat, saturated fat, cholesterol, carbohydrate, protein, fiber, sodium, and potassium.
- RDIs (Reference Daily Intakes): a set of dietary references based on the Recommended Dietary Allowances for essential vitamins and minerals and, in selected groups, protein. The name "RDI" replaces the term "U.S. RDA."
- RDAs (Recommended Dietary Allowances): a set of estimated nutrient allowances established by the National Academy of Sciences. It is updated periodically to reflect current scientific knowledge.

Nutrition labels—things to look for

- Note the serving size. Many serving sizes may be much less than is actually eaten, so the number of calories and nutrients consumed must be recalculated for real world use.
- Divide the number of calories from fat by the number of total calories to determine what percentage of the total calories is from fat. Any food with more than 30% of its calories from fat may be considered a high fat food. The government defines a low fat food as one that has fewer than 3 grams of fat in a serving, so serving size must be examined carefully.
- Note whether the fats are saturated, unsaturated, or trans fats.
- Whole grain products will be indicated by the word "whole."
- Choose foods that have high fiber content.
- Avoid hidden sugars and eat food low in sugar.
- Review the RDA guidelines listed on the package.

Review Video: Nutrition for Personal Trainers
Visit mometrix.com/academy and enter code: 293901

Exercise Prescription and Programming

Modifications during initial fitness assessment

Certain clients may require modifications in order to complete the initial fitness assessment. If a client has a disease that affects his range of motion or ease of movement, it may be more beneficial to modify assessments or skip some assessments because the risk of injury outweighs the benefit to the client. In addition, clients who are obese may not be able to complete assessments for muscular endurance and strength or flexibility due to their weight. In such cases, it is acceptable to begin with the recommendations allowed for their population group.

Functional fitness and sports-specific training

Functional fitness refers to fitness exercises that easily translate to real life experiences and help avoid injury in those situations. For instance, for a client who experiences low back pain whenever she does things during the day that require twisting of the spine, it is helpful for the personal trainer to incorporate movements that require twisting of the spine through different planes of movement and with varying resistance modalities to strengthen that area and train it in a new movement pattern. Sports-specific training emphasizes speed, strength, power, and endurance in athletic situations and also includes training specific to the sport in which the client participates. The average client does not necessarily need to engage in sports-specific training.

Balance training

Balance training becomes more important as clients age, and is especially important if clients have diseases such as arthritis. Balance can be included as a separate section of the workout, or if the client is more advanced, it can be combined with other exercises. An example of balance training can be to simply balance on one leg for a certain amount of time. An example of a combined balance and resistance move could be to do a one-legged bicep curl. In addition, balance can be included in cardiovascular training by having clients walk up and down stairs without the use of the railing or walking backwards on an indoor track. Modifications for balance exercises can include providing support for the client by allowing him to hold on to the personal trainer's arm, wall, or railing.

Sports-specific training in power and strength

Sport-specific training for power tends to emphasize explosive movements. This can be achieved through jump training (plyometrics) and through resistance training. Such examples would include jumping hurdles or doing jump squats, and using lighter weights but lifting as quickly or "explosively" as possible. Understanding the anaerobic system allows the personal trainer to work for the goal of power more effectively by utilizing rest periods to full capacity. Strength training involves methodically increasing weight while doing fewer repetitions in order to gain strength. For sports-specific strength the entire body is worked, but the muscles needing to be strengthened for sports performance are given special attention.

Anaerobic vs. aerobic training

Aerobic training uses oxygen to convert food nutrients (primarily carbohydrates) into usable energy. Any time exercise continues after 2 minutes, the aerobic system kicks in. The anaerobic system is the first responder to exercise, and it also converts food nutrients (primarily carbohydrates) into a fuel source, but it does not use oxygen to do so. Anaerobic exercise can refer to short bouts of activity and includes resistance and plyometric training. Aerobic exercise tends to refer to endurance activities such as running or bicycling.

Precautions to take during extreme weather conditions

When extreme weather conditions are present, special care should be taken if exercise testing or training must take place outside. If conditions are hot and humid, it is important that the clients are well-hydrated prior to beginning exercise and are given plenty of opportunities to re-hydrate during exercise. They should be wearing clothing that is moisture-wicking and avoid wearing cotton if at all possible. Clients should be given adequate rest periods. Clients should be observed for signs of heat stroke or heat exhaustion. When conditions are cold and humid, the same instructions apply but with a few modifications. Clients should layer clothing that is moisture-wicking so they can remove it as their body warms up. Additionally, the warm-up should be lengthened to warm up the muscles adequately. In either situation, personal trainers should monitor the clients closely, as they will not always be assertive when they need hydration or if they feel light-headed or dizzy.

Training at moderate and high altitudes

At higher altitudes, it is important to ensure that clients remain hydrated. When a client feels cold, she may not necessarily feel thirsty. Higher altitudes can quickly cause dehydration if the client is waiting until she feels she needs a drink. Feelings of fatigue can also be increased as less oxygen is binding to the hemoglobin molecules in the client's blood. Frequent breaks may be in order, and if the client is traveling to moderate or high altitude and intends to exercise, she must be aware that she may not be able to exercise at the same capacity. She also needs to schedule water breaks even when she is not thirsty. It is important to drink water throughout the day so she is adequately hydrated for her exercise session.

Recording client progress

Recording client progress at the end of each exercise session gives the personal trainer a small picture of how the client is doing from session to session. At the time of reassessment and re-testing, the trainer can then compare results with session notes. This gives both the trainer and the client a full picture of progress. In addition, if keeping in contact with a cooperating physician, it is necessary for the personal trainer to provide ample documentation for liability reasons and so the physician stays as informed as possible.

Choosing appropiate exercises for specific goals

The personal trainer bases each exercise session around one or more of the client goals. With primary goals, it may be necessary to center the entire session around that one goal. With secondary goals, it may be effective to group them together for a session. The client will be more invested in each workout if he knows what goals are being worked on and why. If he can see how the exercises he is doing will help him reach his goals, he will also have increased motivation to continue faithfulness to the exercise routine.

Review Video: 4 Tips for Setting Great Client Goals
Visit mometrix.com/academy and enter code: 175935

Program design and session and long-term goals

Program design must be specific to where the client's current level of fitness lies. It will not be a beneficial experience for either the client or the trainer if session goals and long-term goals do not match. Session goals should be building blocks that help the client reach the overall goals and thus must be closely related to the overall goals. The program design must properly reflect both the session and overall goals. It is beneficial for the trainer to recognize in both written and verbal form the specific goals for each session.

Interval, continuous, and circuit training programs

Interval training for cardiovascular fitness involves changing speed or grade at various time intervals at which the activity is performed. Continuous training involves staying at a similar speed or grade throughout the entire activity, and circuit training combines cardiovascular and resistance training. Each of these three types of training can be advantageous for cardiovascular fitness. For individuals who were previously sedentary, continuous training is helpful when it is maintained at low to moderate intensities because it will build their endurance, encourage weight loss, and condition their heart rate. Interval training can provide challenges and increase caloric expenditure while still training the client's cardiovascular system. Circuit training combines resistance activities with cardiovascular activities and helps build strength as well as endurance. The drawbacks to these types of training are similar to anything else; if continued for too long, clients will reach a plateau in their performance. Additionally, if one is emphasized over the others, cardiorespiratory fitness or muscular fitness may suffer.

Interval and circuit training could be disadvantageous for a client if the primary goal is to increase her endurance. When doing these types of activities, the client may have to stop the exercise sooner than if a continuous mode of activity was used because the intensity is more difficult. If endurance is the primary goal, it should be attended to first. As endurance increases, interval or circuit training may become more appropriate to include in the training regimen.

<u>Energy systems used</u>

In continuous training, the aerobic system is the primary responder. It is also the primary energy system used in interval training, provided there is no break taken between intervals. With circuit training, either the anaerobic or aerobic system can provide the primary source of energy. When circuit stations are done for less than 2 minutes with at least 30 seconds to 1 minute of rest between stations, anaerobic pathways supply the energy through the ATP-PC and glycolytic pathways. If stations are rotated with less rest, or clients stay at the station for more than 2 minutes, the aerobic system becomes the primary energy pathway.

<u>Rest within circuit training</u>

In circuit training, rest performs a very important function if the goal is to tax the anaerobic system and cause it to be the primary function. The rest periods between stations cause the anaerobic system to "reload" and be ready to function in the next set of exercises. It is important for the personal trainer to understand that rest plays a large part in the training of the anaerobic system.

Relation of ADLs to long-term fitness goals

When the personal trainer is assessing and creating long-term client goals, it is important to assess how the client feels about his normal life activities. The personal trainer can question him about his leisure time, whether he feels he is physically able to do what he enjoys, or whether any common activities (i.e., sitting or standing for long periods of time) cause unnecessary discomfort. The personal trainer must incorporate exercises that address these issues as they directly correlate to the client's quality of life. Increasing his quality of life allows the client to see that exercise can enable him to do what he enjoys, and it helps him desire to continue seeing those benefits. Activities of daily living can have both short- and long-term goals that relate to them.

Activity and training recommendations for different goals

For general cardiovascular and strength benefits, clients can follow the general guidelines for cardiovascular and muscular fitness and flexibility. For losing weight, it is recommended that clients expend at least 2000 kcal per week in physical activity. For gaining weight, clients need to focus on resistance training for hypertrophy. In addition, for both clients who wish to lose weight and who wish to gain weight, diet plays an important role. In losing weight, caloric ingestion must be regulated and decreased from when they were sedentary. In gaining weight, caloric ingestion must be increased, but it must come from nutritious foods. To improve fitness level and increase athletic performance, clients can focus on specific variables, such as hypertrophy, power, endurance, and speed training as best fits their personal goals. The key with this type of clients is to make sure each workout is challenging and not too comfortable for them.

Advanced methods of resistance training

When a client has given evidence that she is ready for advanced forms of resistance training, the personal trainer can introduce methods such as super sets, Olympic-style lifts, plyometrics, pyramid training, drop set training, contrast training, complex system, lactate tolerance system, or negative set system. Only when the client has moved easily from easy to complex movements in traditional resistance training models should she move on to more difficult resistance training. Olympic-style movements train clients for quick, explosive movements that lift heavier weights. Plyometrics, also known as "jump training," trains for speed and power through different styles of explosive jumps. Pyramid sets begin with high volume and low weight, then increase to low volume with high weight through each subsequent set. Drop set training is a system that uses the same exercise performed to volitional failure in one set, then the weight is lowered and the exercise is repeated. Contrast training combines strength and power training by completing one exercise until volitional failure; a similar movement is then per-formed with a lighter weight but faster pace. Complex training com-bines agonist/antagonist exercises to fatigue a certain muscle in or-der to encourage hypertrophy. The lactate tolerance system has the goal of finishing a predetermined workout in the shortest amount of time possible. The negative set system encourages the exerciser to lift a heavier weight than normal, control the eccentric contraction, and have a spotter assist her with the concentric contraction.

Fitness components related to motor skill

Agility refers to a client's ability to explosively perform several different power movements one after another and in opposing directions; for example, zigzagging. Balance refers to a client's ability to control his body position while either standing still or moving. Reaction time means the client is able to react quickly to exercise stimulus or verbal instruction and change his movement pattern accordingly. Speed is quickness of movement, and power refers to explosive contractions of the muscles. Coordination is the client's ability to do all the aforementioned components so that effective movement occurs.

Contraindications for squats, planks, reverse crunches, and plyometrics

If a client has bad knees or shoulders or back, is morbidly obese, and is unfamiliar with exercise in general, the following types of exercises should be avoided: squats, planks, reverse crunches, plyometrics. Clients need to be started with exercises that are simple before moving on to exercises that are more complex. In addition, clients may need the extra core support that standard resistance machines give before moving on to body-weight exercises that are unsupported. Beginning with these sorts of exercises increases the risk for unnecessary injury.

Contraindications for yoga, PNF, static stretching

Yoga might be contraindicated if the client has greatly reduced flexibility, has an injury, or has had joint or back surgery. In these instances, it is wise to consult the client and assess whether the potential benefit would outweigh the risk. PNF or static stretching might be contraindicated for the client if joints are inflamed; if stretching causes excessive pain; or if she currently has an infection, a vascular or acute injury, joint instability, or a disease that affects the tissue being stretched. If in doubt, consult medical personnel before beginning a stretching regimen.

Contraindications for high-intensity, high-impact cardiovascular exercises

High-intensity, high-impact cardiovascular exercises should be avoided in clients if they have a chronic disease that compromises their joints, an acute injury, acute infection or sickness, or if in general the client has any physical issues that may be exacerbated by beginning a high-intensity regimen. For most clients, moderate physical activity is sufficient for health benefits and disease reduction. The personal trainer must assess the benefits/risk ratio for his client.

Recommendations for overall fitness

Healthy adults and seniors

In general, the client should engage in cardiorespiratory activity 3–5 days/week, resistance training 2–3 days/week, and flexibility (ideally) 5–7days/week. Each activity should emphasize the major muscle groups. Cardiorespiratory training should occur ideally at a range of 12–16 on the RPE scale, and resistance exercise should occur at a range of 19–20 RPE with the intent to reach volitional failure. Stretches should be held for 15–30 seconds each, with each muscle group being stretched 2–4 times at each session.

Healthy children and adolescents

Children should accumulate 60 minutes to several hours of moderate and vigorous physical activity on most days of the week. There should be several periods of activity during the day that last 15 minutes or more, and all activities should be age appropriate. Extended periods of activity that last longer than 2 hours are not encouraged during the day due to heat considerations.

Healthy pregnant women

In pregnant women who are healthy, 30–40 minutes of physical activity on most to all days of the week are encouraged. Women who were sedentary prior to becoming pregnant can begin an exercise regimen that is light. Exercise in the supine position after the first trimester should be avoided due to slightly obstructed venous return that lowers cardiac output and could cause orthostatic hypotension.

Adults with cardiovascular disease but medically cleared to exercise

If clients have a chronic heart disease that is stable, they generally need an extended warm-up (5–10 minutes), resistance exercises 2 days/week that include all the major muscle groups (clients should perform 1 set of 10–15 repetitions to moderate fatigue and use 8–10 different exercises; weight should be increased at a rate of 2–5 lbs per week for arms and 5–10 lbs per week for legs), and cardiovascular activity 3–4 times weekly (in addition to an increase in daily total energy expenditure) that is moderate intensity. For the greatest benefits, 5–6 hours of cardiovascular activity per week is recommended. Stretching all the major muscle groups (15–30 sec each, 2–4 stretches per muscle group) daily is encouraged.

Adults with metabolic syndrome but medically cleared for exercise

For clients who have a metabolic syndrome but are medically cleared for exercise, their goals should include the following: cardiorespiratory activity 3–4 days/week, lasting 20–60 minutes, at an intensity of 50–80% of their HRR. Resistance training should emphasize lower resistance and lower intensity: 1 set of 10–15 repetitions for each of the major muscle groups, increasing to 15–20 repetitions. Stretching of all the major muscle groups (15–30 sec each, 2–4 stretches per muscle group) should be emphasized on a daily basis.

Adults with chronic pain and arthritis but medically cleared to exercise

For adults who suffer from arthritis or other joint pain, their exercise prescription is as follows: cardiorespiratory (3–5 days/week, 20–60 min duration, large muscle groups emphasized), resistance (2–3 days/week, 1 set of 3–20 repetitions, 8–10 total exercises that cover all the major muscle groups), flexibility (preferred: 5–7 days/week, 15–30 sec each, 2–4 stretches for each major muscle group). Overstretching should be discouraged; morning exercise depends on a client-by-client basis, based on whether they find it helpful or not.

Exercise modifications

When an exercise is too challenging or not challenging enough, the personal trainer should give a modification that will make it more appropriate for the client. It is the personal trainer's responsibility to observe the client and ask questions to make sure the intensity or the type of exercise is appropriate for the client; some clients have a "pain is gain" mentality and may not volunteer that the exercise is too difficult for them. Likewise, clients new to exercise may not realize if an exercise is too easy for them; they may simply appreciate that they don't feel horrible as they exercise. The personal trainer must educate her clients on the benefits of an appropriately challenging workout.

Components and appropriate flow of an exercise program

An exercise session should start up with an adequate warm-up of the large muscle groups that will also increase the heart rate and prepare the body for what is to come. Depending upon the client, static stretches may be appropriate after the warm-up. Resistance activity should come next, so the client is not too fatigued to be paying attention to proper technique, appropriate weight choice, and personal trainer cues. Next should come cardiovascular activity, followed by a cool-down, and static stretches.

Exercises for major muscle groups

The following exercises would be appropriate for the major muscle groups: chest (push-ups), upper back (double arm row), abdominal muscles (abdominal curl-ups), lower back (good morning), quadriceps group and hamstring group (weighted squats), calves (calf raises), shoulders (shoulder raises), biceps (biceps curls), and triceps (triceps dips).

Monitoring response to exercise

During exercise, there are various ways that a personal trainer can monitor a client's response to exercise. The RPE scale is an efficient way of assessing whether the workload is too challenging or not challenging enough for the client. Paying attention to physical signs of distress, such as labored breathing, pallor, dizziness, or sharp pain, can also be indicators that something more serious may be occurring.

Maximum heart rate and heart rate reserve

In order to find the maximum heart rate, simply take the client's age and subtract it from the number 220. The resulting number is the age-adjusted maximum heart rate. To find the heart rate reserve (HRR), take the client's age and subtract it from 220. Take the resulting number, and subtract the resting pulse from it. This is the heart rate reserve. If training according to a percentage of the client's heart rate reserve, multiply the HRR by the percentage desired for training, then add the resting pulse to it. **Example:** A 60-year-old client needs to be trained at 70% of his HRR, his resting pulse is 65: 220 – 60 (age) = 160 (age-adjusted maximum heart rate); 160 – 65 (resting pulse) = 95; 95 x .70 = 66.5 + 65 (resting pulse) = 131.5 bpm. This client should have the goal of 131 bpm for training at 70% of his HRR.

Target heart rates for different medical considerations

Depending on the chronic condition that the client has, a specific training zone will be based on her HRR. Cardiac patients should have a goal of training up to 85% of HRR. For managing hypertension, training from 40% to 70% of HRR is recommended. For clients with arthritis, it is recommended to train within 50% to 85% of HRR. Diabetic clients should train within 50% to 80% of HRR. For clients with dyslipidemia, it is recommended to train within 40% to 70% of their HRR. For obese clients, initial exercise should have the goal of being within range of 40% to 60% of HRR; progression to higher intensities (50% to 75% of HRR) is recommended. For clients with osteoporosis, it is recommended to pursue non-impact activities at 40% to 70% of HRR.

Periodized training

Periodized training allows the personal trainer to focus on goals such as endurance and hypertrophy with a client while avoiding overtraining. For example, a period of 12 weeks can be broken down into 3 periods of 4 weeks in each period. Through these different periods, the trainer varies the client's intensity, frequency, and duration of exercise so that a plateau is not reached, but maximal hypertrophy and endurance is attained. Chance of injury is reduced because the client is rotating training styles and also which muscles are receiving the most training. Periodized training also helps those clients concerned with increasing different exercise variables such as speed, strength, and power.

In a periodized training schedule, the personal trainer can vary the goal within each period so that muscular power, hypertrophy, endurance, and strength can be achieved without reaching a plateau. For the goal of power, high-intensity, short-interval exercises should be included with the goal of most movements being explosive rather than static. Moderate-intensity sessions should be in between the power sessions to promote recovery. For hypertrophy, resistance training should be with a moderate-intensity weight, 10–15 repetitions, with rest of 30–60 seconds between sets. Endurance activities can be coupled with hypertrophy training and should be between 30–60 minutes for 4–6 days per week at moderate intensity, or 30–60 minutes 2–3 days per week for higher training intensities. Strength training should be done with higher resistance than hypertrophy training. The goal should be 2–3 sets of 6–8 repetitions, where the client feels tired with the last 2 repetitions. Additionally, exercises should be specific to the client's sport goals if they have any.

Review Video: Important Terms
Visit mometrix.com/academy and enter code: 909745

Resistance exercises to build strength

Resistance exercises can help build muscular strength and endurance. When using the proper types of exercises, a client is able to more easily complete activities of daily living, deter rapid bone loss, and reduce the risk for joint disease. Resistance training works along with cardiovascular training to decrease fat mass and increase lean mass. Resistance exercises break down the muscles by creating micro-tears in the tissue; the proper recovery period helps to rebuild those tissues and increase strength and hypertrophy.

Effects of cardiovascular training on activities of daily living and endurance activities

Cardiovascular training helps the heart to pump blood more effectively. As such, resting heart rate begins to lower and resting blood pressure begins to lower. During exercise, heart rate and blood pressure take longer to increase as the body becomes more efficient with the workload. Clients will notice the longer they are committed to an exercise routine, the more daily activities they will be able to complete with less pain or fatigue involved. Clients will also notice better quality of sleep and feel more energetic. For endurance activities, clients will notice that they can exercise for longer periods of time, increase their speed, and overall adapt to training stimulus more quickly.

Effects of exercise on motor skills and coordination

As clients exercise, they will notice a positive effect on motor skills and coordination. With specific training in each of the following areas: resistance, flexibility, cardiovascular, and balance, clients will have increased quality of life. Coordination and motor skills are improved when speed and balance activities are included in the training regimen. Balance training can be incorporated in resistance training (e.g., completing a bicep curl while standing on one leg) or in cardiovascular activities (e.g., power skips or bicycling) and trains clients to use their fine and gross motor skills to complete the movement. The more movements are practiced in an exercise session, the more efficient clients will become in performing them, and their motor skills and coordination will continue to improve.

Demonstration of expected movement patterns

To ensure the client understands exactly what to do for an exercise, the personal trainer needs to physically demonstrate the movement pattern as well as provide verbal and nonverbal cues. It is never appropriate for the trainer to assume the client understands based on verbal instruction alone. An example of a verbal cue is to give instructions for how to complete an exercise. An example of a nonverbal cue would be personally demonstrating the exercise or helping the client complete the movement.

Demonstration of proper range of motion

Demonstrating proper range of motion helps the client to remain free from injury. One resistance exercise that is often done incorrectly is the lat pull. People will typically pull the bar down behind their neck and head. Although the glenohumeral joint can rotate 360 degrees, it is not advisable to train by bringing the arms behind the head in this manner. Proper form requires lowering the bar in front of the face and neck but not leaning back away from the bar. Performing this exercise improperly often leads to overuse injuries in the shoulder joint that could become serious enough for medical attention.

Benefits of using several different resistance modalities

Using several different resistance training modalities allows the trainer to see what the client enjoys the most. This also gives the client a taste of the variety resistance training can offer. Additionally, muscles can be trained in different ways depending on the goal of strength, hypertrophy, endurance, or power, and it becomes less likely that a plateau will occur for the client. Examples of different resistance modalities include the following: variable resistance devices, static resistance devices, kettle bells, dynamic constant external resistance devices, etc. It is necessary for the personal trainer to always keep her eyes on the client during the performance of each movement. Spotting is appropriate and requires verbal and nonverbal cues to ensure the client is performing each movement as safely as possible.

Nontraditional resistance training activity

For some clients, nontraditional resistance training may be in order; this can include stability balls, balance boards, resistance bands, medicine balls, and foam rollers. These pieces of equipment are useful for clients who are rehabilitating from injury, are elderly, are incapacitated in any way, or need to work on their balance. Additionally, it provides a way to change a movement and make it more complex so as to increase the intensity of the workout for clients. Using this type of equipment is also considered functional training and helps clients achieve ease of movement and greater strength in activities of daily living.

Overtraining

The following are signs that the client may be overtraining: fatigue, moodiness, unenthusiastic about workouts, difficulty sleeping at night, and irritation. If these signs are obvious in the client to a great extent, it may be necessary to refer the client to a physician. Overtraining can result from a desire to get in shape faster by exercising longer and harder than is necessary and not utilizing rest periods. It can also be the result of poor self-image or an eating disorder. It is necessary for the personal trainer to educate the client on the dangers of overtraining and how it can be avoided.

Improper form and technique

Using improper technique and form, whether performing cardiovascular or resistance-type activities, can be detrimental to a client's health. It can cause overuse or acute injuries, both of which impede a client's progress in reaching his health goals. Injury may give a client misgivings about continuing an exercise routine and lower his motivation to become healthy if he feels he is just going to be injured. Additionally, improper technique lessens the benefit of the activity being done because the muscles are not being trained in an appropriate fashion. Also, inappropriate motor patterns for the movement are recorded in the client's mind, and he will have to "unlearn" the wrong technique in order to learn the right technique. It is always more beneficial to learn the correct technique the first time.

Appropriate exercise clothing

When exercising in outdoor conditions, the client must pay attention to the appropriate clothing for outside temperatures. If it is hot and humid outside, cotton is not an appropriate clothing choice because it will not wick away excess moisture from the skin. It is best to avoid wearing a hat, as that will also hold in heat. When exercising in a cold environment, the client must layer her clothing and have a moisture-wicking layer closest to the skin. As she gets hot, she can remove clothing accordingly. The appropriate tennis shoe must also be chosen for whether cardiovascular exercise is prescribed or whether speed or resistance training is prescribed. A thinner-soled shoe is required for plyometric or resistance training, and is also more helpful for training in balance issues.

Learning styles

It is important for the personal trainer to remember that the client may not have a learning style that corresponds with his own. In such circumstances, the trainer needs to be informed on how best to train that client in a way that will make sense with her learning style. For instance, a kinesthetic learner may need to not only have verbal instructions, she may need to do a practice try of the movement before actually beginning a set. Additionally, a visual learner will learn best by watching the trainer go through a complete range of motion with the movement, and an auditory learner will rely heavily on verbal cues.

Properly spotting a client

When spotting a client, the personal trainer must stand either behind, beside, or in front of the client. The appropriate position is dependent on the movement being completed. The trainer should ask permission prior to touching the client; all touch should be professional and with the intention of providing assistance for the movement if necessary.

Determining whether an exercise session should end or continue

If a client is working at an intensity higher than is beneficial for him, it can be evidenced by labored breathing, inability to talk, flushed face, or complaint of sharp pain. If an exercise is stopped, the personal trainer needs to assess whether the client can continue working out after a short break. If client heart rate lowers significantly and client feels able to continue, exercise can continue. If the client still feels faint or exasperated following the break, the session may need to be terminated.

Normal and abnormal response to exercise

In a healthy adult, the normal response to exercise is increased heart rate and blood pressure as blood is shuttled to the working muscles. In an adult with chronic health issues, heart rate and/or blood pressure may rise too quickly and cause negative symptoms that may cause the exercise session to be terminated. The personal trainer must make sure adults with chronic conditions begin exercising according to their appropriate protocols.

Improper use of cardiovascular equipment

One example of improper technique when using cardiovascular equipment would be hunching over from the waist or gripping the bar on the treadmill. Both of these issues can cause poor posture and reduce the number of calories being used. Additionally, the client may become light-headed or dizzy because she is compressing her diaphragm by leaning over, which leads to insufficient breath intake and thus hyperventilation to get more air and oxygen to working muscles.

Improper technique for resistance machines, free weights, and stability equipment

When doing any type of resistance activity, form must be prioritized in order to avoid injury. With a resistance machine, any movement that causes the client to arch his back would be an example of improper technique and may indicate that he is using too much weight. For free weight exercises, if the client struggles to complete the move in general, or begins to lean backward in order to complete the movement, this is also improper technique. With stability equipment, any time it is used for something other than its intended purpose to promote balance, it is being used improperly.

Improper stretching techniques

An example of improper technique for partner stretching would be for the partner to force a muscle to stretch farther than it is capable of stretching due to muscle tightness or impaired range of motion. With static stretching, the client must be sure to hold the stretch rather than bouncing in the stretch, as this would promote muscle injury. With dynamic stretching, it would be improper for the client to move a joint outside of its normal range of motion in order to heighten the stretch.

Review Video: Routines
Visit mometrix.com/academy and enter code: 958953

Training Instruction

General exercise principles

- Give verbal cues or directions during exercise.
- Recognize substitution with abnormal movement.
- Modify the parameters to fit the activity.
- Specify your goals from the exercise.
- Start at the level determined by the evaluation.
- Base your activities upon your assessment.
- Demonstrate the exercise you want the client to perform.
- Position the client in a safe position.
- Make sure all joints are in proper position.

Warm-up and cool-down (importance to exercise program)

- *Warm-up* is a short (8-12 minute) period in which a person will stretch the big muscles of the body and move the body less vigorously than he will during the exercise so as to get the body ready to work. A good warm-up may be able to prevent injuries to muscles.
- A *cool-down* is a very short (3-5 minute) time at the end of an exercise period in which the person starts slowing down his or her activity. This lets the blood pressure and circulation normalize and helps to prevent dizziness. At the end of the cool-down, the person may choose to stretch the muscles that were used in the exercise in order to possibly reduce muscle soreness.

Flexibility—definition; benefits practicing flexibility activities

Flexibility is how far a person can move the joints. This ability depends on how far the muscles and connecting tissues can stretch easily, and each joint and joint action will have independent flexibility so that the ability to stretch in one way will not necessarily mean that the person will be able to stretch another way or another area similarly. Flexibility also means how long each muscle and connecting tissue group is when the joint is not moving. Longer muscles mean more flexibility.

- Fewer injuries
- Less muscle tightness
- Less discomfort of the muscles, particularly the back
- Better spinal alignment
- Better ability to react to stimuli
- Lower levels of stress
- Better awareness of the body
- Better capability to do normal tasks

Flexibility guidelines; muscles that are frequently too tight

- The muscles should be warmed up before beginning a stretching activity.
- Start with the biggest muscle groups, do stretches steadily and hold in one position for 15-30 seconds.
- Pay close attention to any muscle groups that may be especially inflexible or do not permit much movement.

- Stretching shows results only in the short-term, so doing flexibility exercises daily, or at least 2-3 times a week, will reveal the most benefits. Flexibility will be reduced if not practiced frequently.
- When doing a stretch, move just until the muscle is tense, but not painful.
- Repeat each stretch 2-4 times.
- Over time, increase the amount of stretch in order to see improvement.
- The upper trapezius, pectoralis major, anterior deltoid, erector spinae (the part in the lumbar spine), iliopsoas, hamstrings, gastrocnemius and soleus are often tight in most people.

Myofascial release; ligament laxity

In myofascial release, the person uses a foam roller to rub an area that is tight and inflexible. This will release the tightness of the tissues surrounding a muscle that may be preventing the muscle joint from reaching its full motion. The tight area is placed over the roller and moved back and forth. When a particularly tense area is reached, the roller is held against the spot for several seconds to let the tissues loosen up. Ligament laxity (sometimes called "double jointedness") is when a person has genetically longer ligaments, thus allowing the joints to be more flexible than they would otherwise be. These people are more prone to injury because of their ability to be able to move into unusual positions.

Cardiorespiratory fitness programs—duration and frequency

- *Duration* is the length of time an exercise is maintained. The current daily exercise recommendation is 20-60 minutes of aerobic activity each day, which can be accumulated in 10-minute periods throughout a day or all at one time. With increased duration of exercise, intensity can be reduced and results will still be seen.
- *Frequency* is the number of days per week a person exercises. A healthy person should exercise 3-5 times per week. Clients who are trying to lose body fat should increase their frequency so as to use more calories. However, exercising more than 5 days per week has not been shown to improve fitness and could increase the likelihood of injury.

Cardiovascular training—overload, intensity, specificity, mode, duration, frequency

- *Overload* is the concept of working the body harder, longer, more frequently, or in a different way than it has in the past to increase the efficiency of the cardiovascular system.
- *Intensity* is how hard an activity is done. *Specificity* is the concept that practicing an activity will result in improvement in only that particular activity. It is also called "SAID" (specific adaptations to imposed demands). *Mode* is the kind of exercise that a person does in order to improve the efficiency of the heart, blood vessels and lungs. *Duration* is the length of time an activity is performed. *Frequency* is the number of times (usually measured per week) that an activity is performed.

Heart, lungs and blood vessels—guidelines for improving efficiency

- *Kind of exercise:* exercises in which bigger muscles are used for an uninterrupted time, and the heart rate is increased.
- *How often:* exercise at least 3 days out of each week. More than 5 days of exercise may not show any improvement.

- *How hard:* exercise at a level in which the heart rate is at 40 to 85% of the HRR (subtract the resting heart rate from the estimated maximum rate the heart will beat). Less fit people should aim for the lower target. Another option is to exercise at 64 – 94% of the estimated maximum rate the heart will beat.
- *How long:* at least 20 minutes per day of exercise, although up to an hour is preferable. Exercise can be in shorter intervals accrued during one day.
- The exercise should also increase over time in how hard it is, and how often and for how long it is performed.

Continuous training and interval training

- *Continuous training* is a routine for improving the efficiency of the heart, lungs and blood vessels by exercising for a long time without resting and at a consistent level of vigor. This may become monotonous for the person exercising, but is simple to learn.
- *Interval training* is a routine for improving the efficiency of the heart, lungs and blood vessels by alternating highly vigorous activity with less vigorous activity during one exercise session. This may be more engaging to the person so that they are more likely to continue with it, and it is easy to increase the level of vigor or the length of time the exercise is performed as fitness is improved.

Fartlek training, super circuit training and cross-training

- *Fartlek training* is a more spontaneous version of interval training in which the person switches between more vigorous activity and less vigorous activity. It is also called speed play training and was developed for running programs, but can be applied to any other cardiovascular fitness activity.
- Super circuit training is a routine for improving the efficiency of the heart, lungs and blood vessels. It involves switching between vigorous aerobic exercise and weight training activities in order to gain muscle fitness and cardiovascular fitness.
- *Cross-training* is a routine for improving the efficiency of the heart, lungs and blood vessels involving practicing a variety of activities over time (either in one session, over one week, or over a year) in order to improve performance in different areas, as well as reduce the rate of injury and increase fitness over a greater range of muscles.

Progression—the three stages

Progression is the concept of increasing the level of activity through three stages in order to eventually reach the point when the person sustains a satisfactory level of fitness over time.

- The *initial conditioning stage* is when a person begins exercising. Exercise programs at this stage should be attainable and motivating, and include a significant period of warming up the muscles, lower intensity activities and a significant period of cooling down the muscles. Exercise may initially be scheduled for as little as 12 minutes, 3 days per week, with an increase over time.
- The *improvement stage* is the stage in which the person is well motivated by the initial success. Exercise should increase in how hard it is, and how long and how often it is performed.
- The *maintenance stage* is the final stage when the person begins to sustain fitness over time.

Muscular fitness—definition; advantages

Muscular fitness is a stage at which the muscle operates efficiently and easily, with increased force and the ability to work for long periods of time. It is the muscle's response to training.

- The body is capable of moving easier and with better efficiency.
- Bones are denser and less likely to develop osteoporosis.
- Insurance against losing muscle as the body ages
- Possible increase in energy usage so that less fat is stored (this may or may not be true, as studies are unclear).
- Tendons and ligaments are stronger and may be less prone to injury
- Better ability to carry out various specific muscle tasks
- The person may begin to feel better about himself and his life.

Some muscle training programs such as circuit weight training can result in improved functioning of the lungs, heart, blood vessels and energy metabolism.

Muscular strength, muscular endurance, muscle power, muscle stability, muscle hypertrophy and volume

- *Muscular strength* is how hard a muscle can move at once.
- *Muscular endurance* is how many times a muscle can do a movement or how long a stationary position can be held.
- *Muscle power* is a combination of muscle strength and the speed at which the movement can be done.
- *Muscle stability* is how well a muscle can hold still, which is especially important for abdominal and back muscles involved in standing.
- *Muscle hypertrophy* is a muscle getting larger as it is trained. *Volume* is the number of times a movement is done ("repetitions") multiplied by the amount of force being moved.

Muscle training plan

- Work one group of an activity until exhausted but still able to do the exercise correctly.
- Do each activity 8-12 times.
- Control the forward and reverse motions of the activity in a deliberate way.
- All muscle groups should be exercised 2-3 times each week, but any particular muscle group should not be worked on successive days (rest days are important to muscle fitness and to avoid injury). In addition, try to do a variety of activities for each muscle group.
- A total muscle training plan should include at least 8 activities, working all the biggest muscle groups of the body rather than concentrating on just one or two muscle groups.

Muscle training—sets, repetitions and intensity

- *A set* is doing an activity several times in a row. A single-set program involves repeating the activity until the muscles are too exhausted to continue doing the activity correctly. A multi-set program involves repeating the exercise until the muscle begins to get tired, and then resting for a few minutes, then doing a second set. Both methods have been shown to have similar results.

- *Repetitions* are the number of times an activity is repeated in each session. Programs considered high-intensity will include a number of repetitions that result in the muscle becoming so tired that it will no longer do the exercise (the muscle will recover in a few minutes).
- *Lower-intensity* programs involve doing enough repetitions to make the muscle tired but still able to work.
- *High-intensity* training may be more effective at increasing strength quickly.

Muscle training—frequency, variety, order of exercises and progression

Muscles need rest from a workout, so 2-3 workouts per week with 2 days in between is recommended. To maintain a habit, different muscle groups can be worked on different days with rest for the worked muscle groups. Varying the activities is important for verifying that all muscles are worked, and to provide a more interesting workout, thus reducing the likelihood of boredom or dropping out of the program. The biggest muscle groups are involved in many different movements for different parts of the body, so it is recommended that the biggest muscle groups be worked first. Activities that work multiple muscle groups should be done before activities that work only one group. However, the back and torso muscles will be needed in most other activities and should not be worked too hard early in the program, otherwise other activities will be difficult to perform.

Muscle training—progression and speed

Muscles will adjust to the workload they are given, so over time the workload must increase in order for muscles to continue to become stronger. This is referred to as progressive resistance exercise (PRE). In a double-progressive program, the number of times the activity is repeated is increased over time until the person can perform the activity 12 or more times without difficulty, and then weight is added, the number of repetitions is decreased and the process begins again. Additionally, more challenging activities can be added to the workout in order to capitalize on the person's increasing muscular fitness.

Speed is another way that progression can be used. Performing an activity very fast should be reserved for more experienced people, however. Most people should perform muscle training exercises slowly and deliberately.

Functional training; closed kinetic chain exercise (CKC); open kinetic chain exercise (OKC)

- *Functional training* means developing a muscle fitness program that improves the ability to perform normal daily tasks.
- *Closed kinetic chain exercises* (CKC) are activities that are similar to actions performed in the life of an average person. These activities are usually done with the feet on the floor.
- *Open kinetic chain exercises* (OKC) are activities that segregate muscle groups in a way that is not typical for daily tasks. Often machines are used for these types of activities. Most people who are not athletes should do more closed kinetic chain exercises. Senior citizens and unfit people will benefit the most from this type of functional training.

Pyramid system; super-slow training system; cheat system of training

- The *pyramid system* involves increasing or decreasing weights and repetitions in one training session. An ascending pyramid system involves lifting more weight while decreasing the number of times the weight is lifted. A descending pyramid involves starting with the most weight the person can lift one time, and then lifting less weight more times with each set. The complete pyramid system is a combination of these two systems, lifting more weight fewer times until the person reaches his maximum weight, and then lifting less weight more times.
- *Super-slow training* involves doing an activity very slowly, pausing at the peak of the resistance, and then returning very slowly.
- The *cheat system* involves doing an activity correctly until the muscles are completely exhausted, then doing the activity incorrectly a few more times, allowing gravity or other muscles to complete the activity.

Pre-exhaustion system; priority training; split routine system; blitz system

- The *pre-exhaustion system* involves doing activities that use bigger muscle sets before activities that use big and small muscle sets. Smaller muscles will tire before bigger muscles, so if the bigger muscles are not somewhat tired before doing the combined activity, the person will have to stop lifting when the smaller muscles get tired and the bigger muscles will not work to their maximum capacity. If the muscles do not work to maximum capacity, they cannot be overloaded, and improvements in strength are not likely.
- *Priority training* focuses on working smaller, less strong muscles at the beginning of an exercise session.
- The *split routine system* alternates working muscle groups on different days so that the person works out every day, but some muscles will rest on any given day. The *blitz system* is similar to a split routine, but each session focuses on only one particular part of the body.

Circuit training, super-circuit training, partial repetitions, forced repetitions, eccentric training

- *Circuit training* involves moving from one activity to another without a break. The person does one set of each activity with moderate vigor.
- *Super-circuit training* involves alternating weight training with cardiovascular exercises.
- The *partial repetitions* system (or "burn system") involves the person working as hard as she can in complete motion activities, then doing variations of those activities while only partially completing the movement.
- The *forced repetitions* system involves the person working as hard as she can on an activity, then a trainer steps in to help her repeat the activity a few more times.
- *Eccentric training* (or "negative training") involves working opposing muscle groups harder. Either a special machine increases the weight on the return (eccentric) part of the activity, or the trainer will help the person lift the weight on the main part of the activity, then let go for the return part.

Considerations for Special Populations

Pregnancy and training

The effects pregnancy can have on the body that may affect her training activities in the following ways:

- Stress on the hips and lower back, along with a higher risk of falling.
- Nerve pain due to swelling, such as carpal tunnel syndrome.
- Increased amounts of blood.
- Faster rate of heartbeat and higher blood pressure
- Pressure from the uterus on the blood vessel running to the heart from the legs
- Less room for the diaphragm, so some difficulty breathing may occur
- Increase in the diameter of the ribcage
- Higher metabolism and warmer body temperature (but less ability to stand heat)
- Feeling tired and sick
- Separation of the muscles in the abdomen
- Increased flexibility of the tissues around joints
- Digestive problems
- Insomnia
- Increased emotional sensitivity
- Increased likelihood of varicose veins

The benefits of exercise during pregnancy include better blood flow, sleep patterns and digestion. Women also may have a better ability to bear their increased weight due to stronger muscles, may feel more lively, fewer back and muscle pains, and gaining less weight. Pregnant women who stay active are less likely to contract gestational diabetes and pregnancy-induced hypertension (PIH).

The risks and concerns of exercise for pregnant women include not gaining enough weight and thus restricting the growth of the fetus, too-high body temperature which may lead to birth defects, possible redirection of the blood flow or glucose away from the fetus during exercise. In general, however, most women should consider an exercise program during pregnancy.

Women who should not exercise during pregnancy without a doctor's clearance include those who have very low levels of iron in the blood, heart murmurs, chronic bronchitis, type 1 diabetes or high blood pressure that is not well-managed, or a diagnosis of intrauterine growth restriction. In addition, women who are very overweight or underweight should be cleared by a physician before exercise. Women who smoke, have seizures, or overactive thyroid should not exercise unless cleared by a doctor.

Some women should definitely not exercise during pregnancy, if they have a diagnosis of heart or lung disease, a cervix that will not stay closed, are carrying more than one baby, are at risk for pre-term labor, have had bleeding in the last 2 trimesters, have been diagnosed with placenta previa after week 26 of the pregnancy, have a broken bag of waters, or a diagnosis of PIH.

Most pregnant women should exercise for at least 30 minutes a day of medium intensity exercise with the following guidelines:

- Avoid exercises in which the risk of injury is high, including activities in which the belly is at risk, or any activities at very low or very high elevations.
- If beginning an activity program for the first time, the best method is to begin in the second trimester with a very low intensity workout.
- Women should listen to their bodies and not do more than they feel they should.
- Drink extra water during activity.
- Progression is not necessary during pregnancy, only that the woman maintains a level of fitness rather than increasing her activity level over the course of the pregnancy.
- Stop exercising if vaginal bleeding begins, the fetal movements decline, if you are feeling faint, if the bag of waters breaks or leaks, or if contractions begin.

Over 65 exercise programs

Considerations for people over 65 and exercise programs are:

- Older people may come to a new exercise program with certain problems:
- The blood vessels may be less elastic and the heart fills with blood slower, so the heart cannot beat as fast as in younger people.
- Older adults use oxygen less efficiently.
- Blood pressure may be higher.
- Older adults may use more medicines.
- Reflexes and reactions are slower.
- Risk of having weaker, porous bones and the disintegration of cartilage, making knee and back injuries more likely.
- Higher body fat and less strength in the muscles
- Stiff joints and higher risk of injury.
- Reduced working of the kidneys, so possibility of dehydration.

The benefits of exercise for older adults are:

- Stronger muscles
- Lower loss of bone
- Improved flexibility and movement
- Better poise and less risk for falling
- Better use of oxygen
- Lower body fat
- Better use of insulin and glucose
- Less risk of atherosclerosis

Older adults

Considerations for older adults beginning an exercise program are:

- Be sure the person is cleared by a doctor.
- When testing fitness, make sure to use age-appropriate standards.
- As with all people, remember that some elderly people will be highly unfit, while others may be very fit, with every stage in between.

- Begin slowly and progress slowly.
- Warm up and cool down for longer periods.
- For those who are weak or inflexible, avoid weight-bearing activities. For those without such problems, begin weight training slowly.
- Moderate the workout if arthritis pain occurs.
- Most elderly people should focus on activities that will make daily tasks easier, focusing on flexibility exercises.
- Work with the physician to get recommendations for the intensity of the workout.
- The primary goal should be to motivate the person to exercise for life, so notice anything that may demotivate them, such as pain, doing too much, or engaging in activities the person doesn't like.

Review Video: Exercise and Special Cases
Visit mometrix.com/academy and enter code: 690677

Children under 12

Considerations for children under 12 beginning an exercise program are:

- Children should be active throughout the day, not sitting for more than 2 hours.
- Activities should be right for the age of the child. As they get older, they should do a more extended 30+-minute activity on most days.
- Children should be active for at least an hour a day total, and having many short-term activities (15 minutes) throughout the day is ideal.
- Weight training should be moderate and children should not try to compete with each other for lifting weights.
- Because they are more likely to overheat, be sure children drink a lot of water and do not stay in the heat too long while doing an activity.

NCSF Practice Test

1. The joint movement that results in an increase of the joint angle is called
    a. Abduction
    b. Adduction
    c. Extension
    d. Flexion

2. Which of these muscles is not part of the Rotator cuff?
    a. Supraspinatus
    b. Infraspinatus
    c. Teres minor
    d. Teres major

3. Which of the following should bc considered a life-threatening medical emergency?
    a. Anterior cruciate ligament tear
    b. A dislocation of the cervical spinal cord
    c. An Achilles' tendon rupture
    d. A hip fracture in an elderly individual

4. Which of the following can cause pain in the lumbar area?
    a. Strain of the tibialis anterior muscle
    b. Strain of the longissimus thoracis muscle
    c. Strain of the gastrocnemius muscle
    d. Strain of the sternocleidomastoid muscle

5. When working with a trainer, an individual lifts a 10-pound weight straight over her head through a distance of 2.5 feet. How much linear work has been generated?
    a. 4 pound-feet
    b. 7.5 pound-feet
    c. 25 pound-feet
    d. 50 pound-feet

6. For average groups of people represented below, which order represents the lowest resting heart rate to the highest resting heart rate?
    a. Men, women, children, elderly individuals
    b. Children, women, elderly individuals, men
    c. Elderly individuals, women, men, children
    d. Elderly individuals, men, women, children

7. The body recruits type I muscle fibers for activities of
    a. long duration and low intensity
    b. long duration and high intensity
    c. short duration and high intensity
    d. none of the above

8. All of the following classes of nutrients provide sources of energy EXCEPT

a. proteins
b. vitamins
c. fats
d. carbohydrates

9. A nonathlete who weighs 80 kg would require ________ grams per day of protein.

a. 50 grams
b. 80 grams
c. 64 grams
d. 100 grams

10. A deficiency of which vitamin can lead to difficulty seeing at night and an increased susceptibility to infections?

a. vitamin B1
b. vitamin B3
c. vitamin E
d. vitamin A

11. You are exercising outdoors and become concerned that your client may be dehydrated. At what point would her condition be considered a medical emergency?

a. When she complains that her leg muscles are cramping
b. When she seems to be confused and doesn't know where she is
c. When she becomes dizzy and light-headed
d. When she begins complaining of a headache

12. What food information is NOT present on a food label?

a. amount of protein in a serving
b. amount of cholesterol in a serving
c. amount of calories in a serving
d. amount of caffeine in a serving

13. When meeting with a client for the first time, all of the following can be helpful comments to make to a client EXCEPT

a. "How would you like this work to help you?"
b. "Can you tell me about your daily routine?"
c. "What health problems do you have?"
d. "Do you think you have clinical depression?"

14. A client in the precontemplation stage of behavior might think to himself:

a. "I just can't lose weight."
b. "I have a plan to lose weight."
c. "I am really thinking about how to lose weight."
d. "I am so proud I lost weight!"

15. An example of a substitution behavioral change that you might suggest to a client is

a. "Call your best friend to walk with you every day."
b. "Take the stairs instead of the elevator at work."
c. "If you reach this goal we set up, you can have a reward of your choosing."
d. "Put your running shoes right by your bed so you are motivated to run first thing in the morning."

16. Your client is in the maintenance stage of behavior and is exercising regularly. One day she cancels her appointments with you, claiming she has too much to do at work. If she abandons her exercise routine completely, it is called a

a. lapse
b. self-change
c. relapse
d. self-challenge

17. All of the following can help the client-trainer relationship EXCEPT

a. Accepting your client for what she is able to do, even if others her age are able to do more
b. Asking your client about his week
c. Answering a text or phone call during a session
d. Keeping information between the two of you confidential

18. An example of active listening is

a. "Why didn't you do this exercise this week?"
b. "Great job with your exercises this week!"
c. "How did your big project at work turn out?"
d. "So you are saying that you didn't understand how this exercise was supposed to feel?"

19. The interactive tool that can lead to change by creating an equal partnership between the client and the trainer is called

a. Motivational interviewing
b. Generative moments
c. Appreciative inquiry
d. Change talk

20. Goals that a trainer helps a client set should be all of the following EXCEPT

a. Time-limited
b. Action-based
c. Broadly defined
d. Measurable

21. Active listening, building rapport, and showing understanding of a client's situation are all components of

a. Nonverbal communication
b. Intrinsic motivation
c. Extrinsic motivation
d. Client-centered techniques

22. As a prelude to creating a personal training package for a client, a trainer should obtain all of the following EXCEPT

a. Approval and signature of a physician
b. Informed consent from the client
c. Permission to post the client's photo on the trainer's Web site
d. Health history of the client

23. A number of atherosclerotic cardiovascular disease risk factors exist. A client who has which of the following would be considered to have a positive risk factor for hypertension?

a. Systolic blood pressure ≥ 140 mm Hg on two separate occasions
b. Diastolic blood pressure ≥75 mm Hg on two separate occasions
c. Systolic blood pressure ≥ 140 mm Hg and diastolic blood pressure ≥ 100 mm Hg on one occasion
d. Having taken an antihypertensive medication in the past

24. Shortness of breath at rest is called

a. Ischemia
b. Dyspnea
c. Syncope
d. Orthopnea

25. All of the following are true of intermittent claudication EXCEPT

a. People with diabetes have a greater risk of having intermittent claudication.
b. Intermittent claudication does not usually occur when a client stands or sits.
c. Intermittent claudication usually goes away within 10 minutes of stopping an exercise.
d. Symptoms associated with intermittent claudication are reproducible.

26. Which of the following pulses is not commonly used to determine an individual's heart rate?

a. Carotid
b. Brachial
c. Radial
d. Popliteal

27. Normal systolic and diastolic blood pressure measurements (in mm Hg) include which of the following?

a. Systolic 110, diastolic 75
b. Systolic 130, diastolic 70
c. Systolic 140, diastolic 85
d. Systolic 110, diastolic 85

28. An individual weighs 80 kg and is 1.75 meters tall. What range does his BMI fall into?

a. Normal
b. Overweight
c. Obese class I
d. Obese class II

29. The Rockport is a field test that involves
a. Running continuously for 1.5 miles
b. Walking intermittently for 2 miles
c. Stepping up and down continuously for 3 minutes
d. Walking as fast as possible for 1 mile

30. An individual's flexibility can be assessed by which of the following?
a. A one-repetition bench press
b. A sit-and-reach test
c. A push-up test
d. A curl-up test

31. The hip joint is what type of joint?
a. Ball-and-socket joint
b. Hinge joint
c. Cartilaginous joint
d. Pivot joint

32. The primary function of the respiratory system is
a. Delivering nutrients to tissues in the body
b. Regulating the body's pH level
c. Facilitating the exchange of oxygen and carbon dioxide
d. Maintaining fluid volume to prevent dehydration

33. The type of stretching that requires assistance from a personal trainer is called
a. Active stretching
b. Passive stretching
c. Ballistic stretching
d. Static stretching

34. All of the following are benefits of increased flexibility EXCEPT
a. Improved circulation
b. Increased range of motion
c. Improved coordination
d. Increased chance of muscle injury

35. The condition that involves rapid breakdown of muscle tissue due to too much exercise, which can potentially result in kidney failure, is called
a. Myoglobinuria
b. Rhabdomyolysis
c. Dialysis
d. Proteinuria

36. Benefits of nonlinear periodized training programs include all of the following EXCEPT
a. Using a progressive increase in the workout intensity
b. Allowing for variation in the workout intensity
c. Having a "power" training day
d. Training both power and strength of muscles within one week

37. What is the approximate target heart rate for a 50-year-old man in beats per minute (bpm)?

a. 75 to 120
b. 85 to 110
c. 85 to 145
d. 120 to 160

38. An effective cardiorespiratory training program session should include all of these basic components EXCEPT

a. Power phase
b. Cool-down phase
c. Warm-up phase
d. Endurance phase

39. The "talk test" refers to

a. The practice of speaking with your client before a training session to check in with the client
b. The practice of talking with your client during the cool-down phase to see how the session felt.
c. The ability of an individual while exercising to talk or respond to a trainer's questions without gasping for breath.
d. The comfort level of a client to let a trainer know when an exercise is too hard.

40. Individuals with osteoporosis

a. Should not do flexibility training exercises
b. Should avoid twisting or flexing of the spine
c. Should not worry about proper breathing techniques
d. Are not more likely to develop fractures

41. Which of the following inhibits a person's joint flexibility?

a. Having cold muscles
b. Being a woman
c. Having more relaxed muscles
d. Having a more physically active lifestyle

42. Older adults should engage in an aerobic exercise program that provides which of the following?

a. 25 minutes, 3 days a week of mild intensity aerobic activity
b. 30 minutes, 3 days a week of moderate intensity aerobic activity
c. 20 minutes, 5 days a week of vigorous intensity aerobic activity
d. 30 minutes, 5 days a week of moderate intensity aerobic activity

43. Which of the following conditions is an absolute contraindication for exercising during pregnancy?

a. Poorly controlled seizure disorder
b. Ruptured membranes
c. Heavy smoker
d. Poorly controlled hypertension

44. Common complications of diabetes include all of the following EXCEPT

a. Kidney problems
b. Vision problems
c. Hearing problems
d. Peripheral nerve problems

45. How much weight loss is appropriate for an obese individual with a BMI greater than 30?

a. 1 kg a week
b. 2 kg a week
c. 3 kg a week
d. 4 kg a week

46. Which of the following is not covered when obtaining informed consent from a client?

a. Benefits that the client should expect to gain
b. Risks and discomfort that may be associated with the training program
c. Purpose of the training program
d. How much the training program will cost

47. The end of a bone is called the

a. Epiphysis
b. Periosteum
c. Endosteum
d. Diaphysis

48. All are true of a synovial joint EXCEPT

a. The synovial cavity is filled with synovial fluid.
b. A synovial joint can flex and extend.
c. A synovial joint may be supported by ligaments.
d. A synovial joint never contains any other structures inside of it.

49. Leg raises are an example of

a. Hip extension
b. Knee flexion
c. Hip flexion
d. Hip abduction

50. Which function does the autonomic nervous system NOT regulate?

a. Digestion
b. Breathing
c. Running
d. Secretion of hormones

Answer Key and Explanations

1. C: When a joint is extended, the angle of the joint is increased. Flexion is the opposite of extension, and causes the joint angle to decrease. Abduction refers to movement that is directed away from the midline of the body. The opposite of abduction is adduction. Adduction describes movements that are made toward the midline of the body.

2. D: The Supraspinatus is an abductor of the arm. The Infraspinatus and Teres minor are both external rotators. The Subscapularis is the missing muscle of the rotator cuff.

3. B: Any trauma to the neck (or cervical spine) should be considered a medical emergency. When the cervical vertebrae are dislocated or fractured, the spinal column can become unstable. This can potentially lead to paralysis or death. While an Achilles' tendon rupture or anterior cruciate ligament tear is a serious leg/knee injury, respectively, and may be career ending for athletes, either one is not life threatening. A hip fracture or a fracture of the neck of the femur can cause permanent disability, especially in the elderly. However, these are also not usually life threatening.

4. B: The longissimus thoracis muscle is located in the posterior lumbar region. It is part of the erector spinae group. These muscles help maintain posture and provide stability to the spine. Lumbar pain, also called low back pain, is one of the most common causes of disability. About 60 to 80% of the general population will experience it at some point in their lives. Determining the specific cause of lumbar pain may be difficult, but muscle strain, an intervertebral herniated disc, and joint inflammation can all cause lumbar pain. The other muscles are not located in the lumbar region. The sternocleidomastoid muscle is located in the cervical region. Strain to this muscle occurs with "whiplash" injuries. The tibialis anterior muscle is located on the anterior and lateral part of the lower leg. The gastrocnemius muscle is located on the posterior part of the lower leg.

5. C: Multiplying the force times the distance through which the force travels will result in the linear work generated. Ten times 2.5 equals 25.

6. D: Heart rate is the number of times that the heart beats per minute and can be measured by taking a pulse. Average people have a resting heart rate of 60 to 80 beats per minute (bpm). The elderly have a lower resting heart rate than adult men and women. Men have a resting heart rate that is about 10 bpm lower than that of adult women. Children have resting heart rates that are higher than those of adults. When comparing fit to unfit individuals, fit individuals have a lower resting heart rate.

7. A: The body has two types of muscle fibers: type I and type II. Together, these muscle fibers can do all types of tasks. However, the body recruits each type during different activities or specific times of an activity, depending on the type and duration of motion required. Type I muscle fibers, also called slow-twitch fibers, are used for activities of long duration and low intensity, such as those involving endurance. In contrast, type II muscle fibers are employed for high-speed, high-power tasks. These muscle fibers are capable of generating force more quickly than type I muscle fibers.

8. B: Carbon is critical for the energy production process. Proteins, fats, and carbohydrates—which are all sources of carbon—contribute to a number of functions in the body. They help provide energy so that muscles, nerves, and metabolic processes work normally. Energy is measured in calories (cal) or kilocalories (kcal). When individuals exercise, they can "burn" energy more quickly.

Vitamins and minerals are critical for providing essential nutrients that the body needs to maintain normal function; however, they are not a source of energy.

9. C: The average person's daily requirement for protein is 0.8 g/kg. In other words, multiplying 0.8 by the person's weight in kilograms will give the daily amount of protein in grams needed. For this individual, that would be $80 \times 0.8 = 64$ grams. Athletes require more protein each day—about 1.2 to 2 g/kg of body weight. If this individual were an athlete, he or she would require between 96 and 160 grams of protein per day. In addition to these specific recommendations, it is also recommended that protein account for about 12 to 15% of the total calories a person eats each day.

10. D: Vitamin A, known as retinol, is found in foods such as fish liver oils, butter, and egg yolks. It is critical for red blood cell and embryo development and normal functioning of the eyes, the immune system, and the skin. Vitamin B_1 is also called thiamin. A deficiency of this vitamin can lead to beriberi. Symptoms of beriberi can include cardiovascular problems, peripheral neuropathy, and cognitive and psychiatric problems. Vitamin B_3 is also known as niacin; a deficiency of this vitamin can cause a disease called pellagra. Pellagra can cause a skin rash, gastrointestinal symptoms, or cognitive difficulties. If untreated, it can also lead to death. Vitamin E is an antioxidant that augments the immune system. It can help prevent cell membranes from being destroyed by harmful free radicals.

11. B: Dehydration, heat exhaustion, and heat stroke are conditions that are best avoided by encouraging clients to drink either water or sports drinks often. When individuals wait until they feel thirsty to drink, they may already have lost 1 to 2 liters of fluid. A dehydrated individual may feel less energetic and begin to develop muscle cramps. If not treated, an individual can develop heat exhaustion, which may be manifested by headaches and feelings of nausea. If heat exhaustion isn't treated, an individual may suffer from heat stroke. During heat stroke, an individual's body temperature increases, and he or she may become confused or lose consciousness. This is a medical emergency. The patient needs to have her body temperature lowered as quickly as possible.

12. D: Labeling on food packages is helpful in determining a number of characteristics of a food, including the ingredients, serving size, and nutrients present in the food. Food label information is based on a 2,000 calorie diet. It provides the percent daily value for the amount of fats, cholesterol, sodium, potassium, carbohydrates, and protein present in a serving size. While caffeine will be listed as an ingredient if it is present in the food, the specific amount of caffeine will not be listed.

13. D: It is important to remember that coaching is not therapy or mental health counseling. Personal trainers should never diagnose current psychiatric problems. However, it is important to ask a person about their past history—medical and otherwise—so that your sessions can be appropriate and productive. Knowing about a person's daily routine will tell you how active he or she usually is. Asking, "How would you like this work to help you?" can elicit a specific goal that the two of you can work toward.

14. A: There are five stages of behavioral change. Listed in order of unwilling to change to readiness to change, they are precontemplation, contemplation, preparation, action, and maintenance. People in precontemplation often say, "I can't" or "I won't" about being able to change. People in the contemplation stage often say, "I just may change" or "I'm thinking about it." People in the preparation stage have actively decided to take action at some point soon. In the action stage, a person has decided to implement a consistent change, but has been implementing the new behavior for less than six months. If a person has consistently implemented a change for more than six months, he or she is in the maintenance stage.

15. B: There are a number of strategies trainers can employ in order to effect behavior change in a client. Substitution or counterconditioning involves substituting healthy behaviors for unhealthy behaviors. Answer A is an example of social support. Answer C is an example of a reward or reinforcement system. Answer D is an example of environmental control, which is a cue that can precipitate healthy behavior.

16. C: A relapse is when a person stops their positive behavior and, as a result, loses the positive benefits he or she had gained. Many conditions can lead to relapse; work pressures, boredom, and increased travel are only a few. Although similar, a lapse is a temporary stop in positive behavior. Had this client returned after a week or two, her exercise routine would have lapsed, but she would have likely maintained or quickly regained the positive benefits.

17. C: A number of factors can help facilitate a beneficial working relationship between a client and a trainer. These can include being present in the moment, maintaining confidentiality, being interested in your client's life, giving helpful feedback, and treating your client in a positive way. Along those lines, it is important to accept clients at the level they are currently at, rather than comparing them to others.

18. D: Active listening is a technique than enhances communication. It involves conveying what the client says back to the client, so that the individual feels they are being heard and understood. The client tells you how he or she feels or what he or she thinks, and you repeat or paraphrase it back to the individual. This technique provides the opportunity for clarification in the event that the client actually meant something else. When actively listening, it is helpful to let the other speak without interruption and to maintain eye contact and focus on the client.

19. A: Motivational interviewing is based on the idea that change occurs when there is an equal partnership between the client and trainer. While you are a training expert, your client is an expert is his or her own life. Motivational interviewing is used in a client-centered relationship. Generative moments are powerful or negative events that have happened to a client that can spur him or her to change. Appreciative inquiry is a technique in which the trainer asks positive and powerful questions to help the client visualize potential possibilities. Change talk involves language spoken by a client about his or her desire and ability to change their behavior.

20. C: Goals that are most helpful are those that are specific, very well defined, able to be measured, realistic, and have a time constraint on them. The actions a client needs to take should be specifically defined. For example, a goal may be that a client will walk on his treadmill at a pace of 3 mph for 30 minutes on Monday through Friday before going to work.

21. D: Client-centered techniques include asking open-ended questions, listening actively, and frequently clarifying what the client says. These can all contribute to building rapport and a strong relationship with a client. Nonverbal communication is that which is expressed and received via nonverbal cues, such as facial expressions, gestures, and the presence or absence of eye contact. Intrinsic motivation is the motivation for change that comes from within. For example, a person may want to lose weight to feel proud or to feel like he can achieve a goal. When people are extrinsically motivated, they are motivated to achieve a goal because of an external factor. For example, someone might want to lose weight to fit into a wedding dress.

22. C: While you should always obtain permission before posting a photo of a client on a Web site, that is not one of the critical initial pieces of information. If medical clearance is necessary, a signature and recommendations from your client's physician should be obtained. In addition, you will need to know your client's past and present medical and health issues to create an appropriate

training plan. You will also need informed consent from your client, demonstrating that he or she understands the risk and benefits of undertaking a training program.

23. A: Hypertension is defined by the Seventh Report of the Joint National Committee on Prevention, Detection, Evaluation, and Treatment of High Blood Pressure as a systolic blood pressure of ≥ 140 mm Hg and a diastolic blood pressure of ≥ 90 mm Hg on two separate occasions. In addition, current use of an antihypertensive medication is considered to be a positive risk factor for hypertension.

24. B: A client with dyspnea will have shortness of breath while resting or only with mild exertion. It is not normal, and it can be a symptom of cardiac or pulmonary disease. Orthopnea is shortness of breath that occurs when one is lying down. It is relieved by sitting upright or standing. Ischemia occurs when there is a lack of blood flow and oxygen to the heart. This causes pain in the chest or pain that has radiated to the neck or arm. Syncope is a loss of consciousness that usually occurs when the brain does not receive enough oxygen.

25. C: When an individual has intermittent claudication, he or she will develop pain in a specific area with exercise due to inadequate blood flow to that specific muscle. This pain can be reproduced from day to day. It usually does not occur when a client is sitting or standing. People with coronary artery disease or diabetes are prone to developing intermittent claudication. However, once the exercise that precipitated the pain has stopped, the pain should go away within one to two minutes.

26. D: The popliteal artery, located behind the knee, can be difficult to palpate. The carotid pulse is felt by placing one's fingers lightly in the lower neck, along the medial aspect of the sternocleidomastoid muscle. The brachial pulse can be palpated between the triceps and biceps muscles on the anterior and medial aspect of the arm, near the elbow. The radial artery can be palpated on the anterior arm, near the wrist.

27. A: Normal blood pressure is classified as a systolic pressure of less than 120 mm Hg and a diastolic pressure of less than 80 mm Hg. If either the systolic or diastolic pressures are elevated on multiple occasions, an individual's blood pressure is considered to be high.

28. B: BMI stands for body mass index, and it can be calculated by dividing an individual's weight by height squared. In this example, BMI = 80 kg / $(1.75\text{ m})^2$. This results in a BMI of 26.1. BMI values fall into a range. The normal range is 18.5–24.9. The overweight range is 25–29.9. The obese class I range is 30–34.9. The obese class II range is 35–39.9.

29. D: The Rockport 1-mile walk test involves having a client walk as fast as he or she can for a distance of 1 mile. The individual must not run at all during this test. At the end of the test, the individual's pulse and heart rate are measured. The Queens College Step Test involves having an individual step up and down on a standardized step height continuously for 3 minutes and then measuring his or her pulse and heart rate after the 3 minutes.

30. B: A sit-and-reach test can measure the flexibility of an individual's lower back, hip, and hamstrings. A one-repetition bench press is used to assess muscular strength or muscle force. Both the push-up test and the curl-up test are used for measuring muscle endurance.

31. A: The hip joint as well as the shoulder joint can move in all directions. They are ball-and-socket joints. A hinge joint can only move in one plane, such as with knee flexion and extension. A cartilaginous joint is a strong joint that is very slightly movable, such as intervertebral joints. A pivot joint is a joint in one plane that permits rotation, such as the humeroradial joint.

32. C: The respiratory system involves the lungs and is where the exchange of oxygen for carbon dioxide occurs. The cardiovascular system, which involves the heart and blood vessels, is responsible for delivering oxygen and nutrients to all tissues in the body, regulating the body's pH level to prevent acidosis or alkalosis, and maintaining fluid volume to prevent dehydration.

33. B: In passive stretching, a client remains relaxed, allowing a trainer to stretch the client's muscles. Ballistic stretching, which involves a bouncing-like movement, can cause injury to muscles if not performed carefully. Static stretching involves movements that are deliberate and sustained. Active stretching involves stretching muscles throughout their range of motion.

34. D: Flexibility training has a number of benefits, including increased circulation, increased range of motion, improved muscle coordination, and decreased future chance of muscle injury.

35. B: Rhabdomyolysis, caused when an individual exercises too excessively, results in muscle damage and breakdown. These breakdown products, which can include protein and myoglobin, then enter the bloodstream and have the potential to harm the kidneys. Kidney failure, and possibly death, can result. Symptoms of rhabdomyolysis can include muscle swelling, pain, and soreness. Myoglobinuria and proteinuria describe the conditions of having myoglobin and protein in the urine. However, they do necessarily reflect a cause. Dialysis is a treatment for kidney failure.

36. A: While a linear periodized training program involves having a progressive increase in the workout intensity over the course of a week, a nonlinear periodized training program involves variation of intensity over the course of a week. A weeklong nonlinear periodized training program can target both muscle strength and power. A "power" training day involving power sets can also be implemented. This type of program may be more conducive to individuals with scheduling conflicts.

37. C: To calculate an individual's target heart rate, first one needs to estimate the person's maximal heart rate. This is estimated by subtracting a person's age from 220. In this example, the person's maximal heart rate is $220 - 50 = 170$. Using this number, the target heart rate can be calculated. The recommended target heart rate is between 50% and 85% of the maximal heart rate. This would be $170 \times 0.50 = 85$, and $170 \times 0.85 = 145$. So, the individual's target heart rate is estimated to be between about 85 and 145 bpm.

38. A: A training program needs to balance many different variables in order to be effective. A trainer needs to take a client's goals, daily routines, and preferences into account to create a routine that will be followed. Each training session should include a warm-up phase, a workout or endurance phase, and then a cool-down phase.

39. C: It is important that a training session not be too intense. The "talk test" is a simple way to get a handle on the intensity of the endurance or workout phase. A client should be able to talk or answer a trainer's questions without gasping for breath. Not being able to speak easily can indicate that the workout is too intense. Cardiovascular, muscular, and orthopedic injuries are more likely to occur when a workout is too intense.

40. B: Osteoporosis is a disease that involves a loss of bone mineral density. Osteopenia is a milder form of osteoporosis. Although people with osteoporosis are more susceptible to fractures due to the thinning of their bones, they are appropriate candidates for flexibility training programs. These programs can help improve posture and maintain the alignment of the spine. However, the program should avoid repetitive exercises that involve twisting or flexing of the spine. Everyone who participates in a flexibility training program should be taught proper breathing techniques.

41. A: A person's flexibility is reflected in his or her ability to move a joint, without pain, through a range of motion. In general, a number of factors are associated with increased flexibility. Younger people are more flexible than older individuals, and women are more flexible than men. Warmer, more relaxed muscles allow more joint flexibility than colder muscles. Individuals who are physically active are often more flexible than those who are not. In addition, the joint structure and health of the joint and its surrounding tissues affect an individual's flexibility.

42. D: If their medical issues allow it, individuals over the age of 65 can and should participate in exercise training programs. Aerobic, or cardiorespiratory, exercise can decrease morbidity and mortality rates in older individuals. The recommendations are for older individuals to engage in moderate intensity aerobic activity for 30 minutes, 5 days a week (150 minutes total), or to engage in vigorous intensity aerobic activity for 25 minutes, 3 days a week (75 minutes total). People can also do a combination of both.

43. B: Recent research supports a role for exercise programs during pregnancy. Goals of this type of program can include reducing low back pain and decreasing the risk for developing gestational diabetes. However, there do exist a number of absolute contraindications. Some of these include ruptured membranes, placenta previa after 26 weeks of gestation, premature labor, preeclampsia, and high-risk multiple gestation pregnancies. In contrast, relative contraindications include the individual being a heavy smoker, having poorly controlled diabetes or seizures, or having poorly controlled hypertension or hyperthyroid disease.

44. C: Diabetes can lead to kidney problems (nephropathy), trouble seeing (retinopathy), and decreased sensation of peripheral nerves (peripheral neuropathy). If these conditions are present, a trainer needs to adapt an exercise program accordingly. Some precautions that can be taken include keeping the blood pressure stable for retinopathy, avoiding exercise requiring high levels of coordination for peripheral neuropathy, or avoiding prolonged exercise for nephropathy.

45. A: People who are obese have a BMI greater than or equal to 30. These individuals are at a high risk of cardiac problems, certain types of cancers, and diabetes. Among other areas, training programs can focus on weight loss, promoting appetite control, and lowering the risk of associated medical issues. Weight loss should be gradual—not more than 1 kg per week. Aerobic training sessions five to seven times a week lasting 45–60 minutes per session may be helpful.

46. D: Obtaining informed consent at the beginning of a professional relationship can protect against potential later legal action. An informed consent document will discuss the reason for the training program, the risks or discomfort that a client may experience, the responsibilities of the client, the benefits the client may reap, and it will offer the opportunity for a client to ask related questions. Fee structure and payments are not part of the informed consent.

47. A: When describing the anatomy of a bone, the epiphysis is the end of a bone and the diaphysis is the shaft of the bone. The periosteum is a membrane that covers the surface of a bone, except at the articular surfaces (joints). The endosteum is the lining of the bone marrow cavity and contains the cells necessary for new bone development.

48. D: A synovial joint is the most common type of joint found in the body and is made up of two articulating bones. Synovial fluid is present in the synovial cavity, which is lined by a synovial membrane. The joint is surrounded by a fibrous capsule, which can be supported by ligaments. Sometimes, a synovial joint may contain other structures, such as menisci (for example, in the knee) or fat pads. There are subtypes of synovial joints, including a hinge joint, ball-and-socket joint, and a pivot joint.

49. C: Leg raises are one type of exercise that works the hip flexor muscles. These muscles include the iliopsoas, rectus femoris, sartorius, and pectineus. Exercises for hip extension include squats or leg presses. Hip extensor muscles are the hamstrings and the gluteus maximus. Hip abduction exercises can be done with an exercise machine. Muscles involved with hip abduction include the tensor fascia latae, sartorius, and gluteus minimus and medius. Leg curl exercises involve knee flexion. Muscles involved with flexion of the knee are the hamstrings, gracilis, and popliteus.

50. C: The central nervous system is comprised of the brain and the spinal cord and is responsible for receiving, analyzing, interpreting, and acting on sensory information. The central nervous system is comprised of the peripheral and autonomic nervous systems. The autonomic nervous system is responsible for functions such as respiration, digestion, making hormones, and maintaining heart rate. The autonomic nervous system can be subdivided into the sympathetic nervous system, which is activated when the body is "stressed" and causes an increase in heart rate and respiratory rate and the parasympathetic nervous system, which is "in control" when the stressful stimulus is no longer present.

How to Overcome Test Anxiety

Just the thought of taking a test is enough to make most people a little nervous. A test is an important event that can have a long-term impact on your future, so it's important to take it seriously and it's natural to feel anxious about performing well. But just because anxiety is normal, that doesn't mean that it's helpful in test taking, or that you should simply accept it as part of your life. Anxiety can have a variety of effects. These effects can be mild, like making you feel slightly nervous, or severe, like blocking your ability to focus or remember even a simple detail.

If you experience test anxiety—whether severe or mild—it's important to know how to beat it. To discover this, first you need to understand what causes test anxiety.

Causes of Test Anxiety

While we often think of anxiety as an uncontrollable emotional state, it can actually be caused by simple, practical things. One of the most common causes of test anxiety is that a person does not feel adequately prepared for their test. This feeling can be the result of many different issues such as poor study habits or lack of organization, but the most common culprit is time management. Starting to study too late, failing to organize your study time to cover all of the material, or being distracted while you study will mean that you're not well prepared for the test. This may lead to cramming the night before, which will cause you to be physically and mentally exhausted for the test. Poor time management also contributes to feelings of stress, fear, and hopelessness as you realize you are not well prepared but don't know what to do about it.

Other times, test anxiety is not related to your preparation for the test but comes from unresolved fear. This may be a past failure on a test, or poor performance on tests in general. It may come from comparing yourself to others who seem to be performing better or from the stress of living up to expectations. Anxiety may be driven by fears of the future—how failure on this test would affect your educational and career goals. These fears are often completely irrational, but they can still negatively impact your test performance.

Review Video: 3 Reasons You Have Test Anxiety
Visit mometrix.com/academy and enter code: 428468

Elements of Test Anxiety

As mentioned earlier, test anxiety is considered to be an emotional state, but it has physical and mental components as well. Sometimes you may not even realize that you are suffering from test anxiety until you notice the physical symptoms. These can include trembling hands, rapid heartbeat, sweating, nausea, and tense muscles. Extreme anxiety may lead to fainting or vomiting. Obviously, any of these symptoms can have a negative impact on testing. It is important to recognize them as soon as they begin to occur so that you can address the problem before it damages your performance.

Review Video: 3 Ways to Tell You Have Test Anxiety
Visit mometrix.com/academy and enter code: 927847

The mental components of test anxiety include trouble focusing and inability to remember learned information. During a test, your mind is on high alert, which can help you recall information and stay focused for an extended period of time. However, anxiety interferes with your mind's natural processes, causing you to blank out, even on the questions you know well. The strain of testing during anxiety makes it difficult to stay focused, especially on a test that may take several hours. Extreme anxiety can take a huge mental toll, making it difficult not only to recall test information but even to understand the test questions or pull your thoughts together.

Review Video: How Test Anxiety Affects Memory
Visit mometrix.com/academy and enter code: 609003

Effects of Test Anxiety

Test anxiety is like a disease—if left untreated, it will get progressively worse. Anxiety leads to poor performance, and this reinforces the feelings of fear and failure, which in turn lead to poor performances on subsequent tests. It can grow from a mild nervousness to a crippling condition. If allowed to progress, test anxiety can have a big impact on your schooling, and consequently on your future.

Test anxiety can spread to other parts of your life. Anxiety on tests can become anxiety in any stressful situation, and blanking on a test can turn into panicking in a job situation. But fortunately, you don't have to let anxiety rule your testing and determine your grades. There are a number of relatively simple steps you can take to move past anxiety and function normally on a test and in the rest of life.

Review Video: How Test Anxiety Impacts Your Grades
Visit mometrix.com/academy and enter code: 939819

Physical Steps for Beating Test Anxiety

While test anxiety is a serious problem, the good news is that it can be overcome. It doesn't have to control your ability to think and remember information. While it may take time, you can begin taking steps today to beat anxiety.

Just as your first hint that you may be struggling with anxiety comes from the physical symptoms, the first step to treating it is also physical. Rest is crucial for having a clear, strong mind. If you are tired, it is much easier to give in to anxiety. But if you establish good sleep habits, your body and mind will be ready to perform optimally, without the strain of exhaustion. Additionally, sleeping well helps you to retain information better, so you're more likely to recall the answers when you see the test questions.

Getting good sleep means more than going to bed on time. It's important to allow your brain time to relax. Take study breaks from time to time so it doesn't get overworked, and don't study right before bed. Take time to rest your mind before trying to rest your body, or you may find it difficult to fall asleep.

Review Video: The Importance of Sleep for Your Brain
Visit mometrix.com/academy and enter code: 319338

Along with sleep, other aspects of physical health are important in preparing for a test. Good nutrition is vital for good brain function. Sugary foods and drinks may give a burst of energy but this burst is followed by a crash, both physically and emotionally. Instead, fuel your body with protein and vitamin-rich foods.

Also, drink plenty of water. Dehydration can lead to headaches and exhaustion, especially if your brain is already under stress from the rigors of the test. Particularly if your test is a long one, drink water during the breaks. And if possible, take an energy-boosting snack to eat between sections.

Review Video: How Diet Can Affect your Mood
Visit mometrix.com/academy and enter code: 624317

Along with sleep and diet, a third important part of physical health is exercise. Maintaining a steady workout schedule is helpful, but even taking 5-minute study breaks to walk can help get your blood pumping faster and clear your head. Exercise also releases endorphins, which contribute to a positive feeling and can help combat test anxiety.

When you nurture your physical health, you are also contributing to your mental health. If your body is healthy, your mind is much more likely to be healthy as well. So take time to rest, nourish your body with healthy food and water, and get moving as much as possible. Taking these physical steps will make you stronger and more able to take the mental steps necessary to overcome test anxiety.

Review Video: How to Stay Healthy and Prevent Test Anxiety
Visit mometrix.com/academy and enter code: 877894

Mental Steps for Beating Test Anxiety

Working on the mental side of test anxiety can be more challenging, but as with the physical side, there are clear steps you can take to overcome it. As mentioned earlier, test anxiety often stems from lack of preparation, so the obvious solution is to prepare for the test. Effective studying may be the most important weapon you have for beating test anxiety, but you can and should employ several other mental tools to combat fear.

First, boost your confidence by reminding yourself of past success—tests or projects that you aced. If you're putting as much effort into preparing for this test as you did for those, there's no reason you should expect to fail here. Work hard to prepare; then trust your preparation.

Second, surround yourself with encouraging people. It can be helpful to find a study group, but be sure that the people you're around will encourage a positive attitude. If you spend time with others who are anxious or cynical, this will only contribute to your own anxiety. Look for others who are motivated to study hard from a desire to succeed, not from a fear of failure.

Third, reward yourself. A test is physically and mentally tiring, even without anxiety, and it can be helpful to have something to look forward to. Plan an activity following the test, regardless of the outcome, such as going to a movie or getting ice cream.

When you are taking the test, if you find yourself beginning to feel anxious, remind yourself that you know the material. Visualize successfully completing the test. Then take a few deep, relaxing breaths and return to it. Work through the questions carefully but with confidence, knowing that you are capable of succeeding.

Developing a healthy mental approach to test taking will also aid in other areas of life. Test anxiety affects more than just the actual test—it can be damaging to your mental health and even contribute to depression. It's important to beat test anxiety before it becomes a problem for more than testing.

Review Video: Test Anxiety and Depression
Visit mometrix.com/academy and enter code: 904704

Study Strategy

Being prepared for the test is necessary to combat anxiety, but what does being prepared look like? You may study for hours on end and still not feel prepared. What you need is a strategy for test prep. The next few pages outline our recommended steps to help you plan out and conquer the challenge of preparation.

Step 1: Scope Out the Test

Learn everything you can about the format (multiple choice, essay, etc.) and what will be on the test. Gather any study materials, course outlines, or sample exams that may be available. Not only will this help you to prepare, but knowing what to expect can help to alleviate test anxiety.

Step 2: Map Out the Material

Look through the textbook or study guide and make note of how many chapters or sections it has. Then divide these over the time you have. For example, if a book has 15 chapters and you have five days to study, you need to cover three chapters each day. Even better, if you have the time, leave an extra day at the end for overall review after you have gone through the material in depth.

If time is limited, you may need to prioritize the material. Look through it and make note of which sections you think you already have a good grasp on, and which need review. While you are studying, skim quickly through the familiar sections and take more time on the challenging parts. Write out your plan so you don't get lost as you go. Having a written plan also helps you feel more in control of the study, so anxiety is less likely to arise from feeling overwhelmed at the amount to cover. A sample plan may look like this:

- Day 1: Skim chapters 1–4, study chapter 5 (especially pages 31–33)
- Day 2: Study chapters 6–7, skim chapters 8–9
- Day 3: Skim chapter 10, study chapters 11–12 (especially pages 87–90)
- Day 4: Study chapters 13–15
- Day 5: Overall review (focus most on chapters 5, 6, and 12), take practice test

Step 3: Gather Your Tools

Decide what study method works best for you. Do you prefer to highlight in the book as you study and then go back over the highlighted portions? Or do you type out notes of the important information? Or is it helpful to make flashcards that you can carry with you? Assemble the pens, index cards, highlighters, post-it notes, and any other materials you may need so you won't be distracted by getting up to find things while you study.

If you're having a hard time retaining the information or organizing your notes, experiment with different methods. For example, try color-coding by subject with colored pens, highlighters, or post-it notes. If you learn better by hearing, try recording yourself reading your notes so you can listen while in the car, working out, or simply sitting at your desk. Ask a friend to quiz you from your flashcards, or try teaching someone the material to solidify it in your mind.

Step 4: Create Your Environment

It's important to avoid distractions while you study. This includes both the obvious distractions like visitors and the subtle distractions like an uncomfortable chair (or a too-comfortable couch that makes you want to fall asleep). Set up the best study environment possible: good lighting and a comfortable work area. If background music helps you focus, you may want to turn it on, but otherwise keep the room quiet. If you are using a computer to take notes, be sure you don't have any other windows open, especially applications like social media, games, or anything else that could distract you. Silence your phone and turn off notifications. Be sure to keep water close by so you stay hydrated while you study (but avoid unhealthy drinks and snacks).

Also, take into account the best time of day to study. Are you freshest first thing in the morning? Try to set aside some time then to work through the material. Is your mind clearer in the afternoon or evening? Schedule your study session then. Another method is to study at the same time of day that you will take the test, so that your brain gets used to working on the material at that time and will be ready to focus at test time.

Step 5: Study!

Once you have done all the study preparation, it's time to settle into the actual studying. Sit down, take a few moments to settle your mind so you can focus, and begin to follow your study plan. Don't give in to distractions or let yourself procrastinate. This is your time to prepare so you'll be ready to fearlessly approach the test. Make the most of the time and stay focused.

Of course, you don't want to burn out. If you study too long you may find that you're not retaining the information very well. Take regular study breaks. For example, taking five minutes out of every hour to walk briskly, breathing deeply and swinging your arms, can help your mind stay fresh.

As you get to the end of each chapter or section, it's a good idea to do a quick review. Remind yourself of what you learned and work on any difficult parts. When you feel that you've mastered the material, move on to the next part. At the end of your study session, briefly skim through your notes again.

But while review is helpful, cramming last minute is NOT. If at all possible, work ahead so that you won't need to fit all your study into the last day. Cramming overloads your brain with more information than it can process and retain, and your tired mind may struggle to recall even previously learned information when it is overwhelmed with last-minute study. Also, the urgent nature of cramming and the stress placed on your brain contribute to anxiety. You'll be more likely to go to the test feeling unprepared and having trouble thinking clearly.

So don't cram, and don't stay up late before the test, even just to review your notes at a leisurely pace. Your brain needs rest more than it needs to go over the information again. In fact, plan to finish your studies by noon or early afternoon the day before the test. Give your brain the rest of the day to relax or focus on other things, and get a good night's sleep. Then you will be fresh for the test and better able to recall what you've studied.

Step 6: Take a practice test

Many courses offer sample tests, either online or in the study materials. This is an excellent resource to check whether you have mastered the material, as well as to prepare for the test format and environment.

Check the test format ahead of time: the number of questions, the type (multiple choice, free response, etc.), and the time limit. Then create a plan for working through them. For example, if you have 30 minutes to take a 60-question test, your limit is 30 seconds per question. Spend less time on the questions you know well so that you can take more time on the difficult ones.

If you have time to take several practice tests, take the first one open book, with no time limit. Work through the questions at your own pace and make sure you fully understand them. Gradually work up to taking a test under test conditions: sit at a desk with all study materials put away and set a timer. Pace yourself to make sure you finish the test with time to spare and go back to check your answers if you have time.

After each test, check your answers. On the questions you missed, be sure you understand why you missed them. Did you misread the question (tests can use tricky wording)? Did you forget the information? Or was it something you hadn't learned? Go back and study any shaky areas that the practice tests reveal.

Taking these tests not only helps with your grade, but also aids in combating test anxiety. If you're already used to the test conditions, you're less likely to worry about it, and working through tests until you're scoring well gives you a confidence boost. Go through the practice tests until you feel comfortable, and then you can go into the test knowing that you're ready for it.

Test Tips

On test day, you should be confident, knowing that you've prepared well and are ready to answer the questions. But aside from preparation, there are several test day strategies you can employ to maximize your performance.

First, as stated before, get a good night's sleep the night before the test (and for several nights before that, if possible). Go into the test with a fresh, alert mind rather than staying up late to study.

Try not to change too much about your normal routine on the day of the test. It's important to eat a nutritious breakfast, but if you normally don't eat breakfast at all, consider eating just a protein bar. If you're a coffee drinker, go ahead and have your normal coffee. Just make sure you time it so that the caffeine doesn't wear off right in the middle of your test. Avoid sugary beverages, and drink enough water to stay hydrated but not so much that you need a restroom break 10 minutes into the test. If your test isn't first thing in the morning, consider going for a walk or doing a light workout before the test to get your blood flowing.

Allow yourself enough time to get ready, and leave for the test with plenty of time to spare so you won't have the anxiety of scrambling to arrive in time. Another reason to be early is to select a good seat. It's helpful to sit away from doors and windows, which can be distracting. Find a good seat, get out your supplies, and settle your mind before the test begins.

When the test begins, start by going over the instructions carefully, even if you already know what to expect. Make sure you avoid any careless mistakes by following the directions.

Then begin working through the questions, pacing yourself as you've practiced. If you're not sure on an answer, don't spend too much time on it, and don't let it shake your confidence. Either skip it and come back later, or eliminate as many wrong answers as possible and guess among the remaining ones. Don't dwell on these questions as you continue—put them out of your mind and focus on what lies ahead.

Be sure to read all of the answer choices, even if you're sure the first one is the right answer. Sometimes you'll find a better one if you keep reading. But don't second-guess yourself if you do immediately know the answer. Your gut instinct is usually right. Don't let test anxiety rob you of the information you know.

If you have time at the end of the test (and if the test format allows), go back and review your answers. Be cautious about changing any, since your first instinct tends to be correct, but make sure you didn't misread any of the questions or accidentally mark the wrong answer choice. Look over any you skipped and make an educated guess.

At the end, leave the test feeling confident. You've done your best, so don't waste time worrying about your performance or wishing you could change anything. Instead, celebrate the successful completion of this test. And finally, use this test to learn how to deal with anxiety even better next time.

Review Video: 5 Tips to Beat Test Anxiety
Visit mometrix.com/academy and enter code: 570656

Important Qualification

Not all anxiety is created equal. If your test anxiety is causing major issues in your life beyond the classroom or testing center, or if you are experiencing troubling physical symptoms related to your anxiety, it may be a sign of a serious physiological or psychological condition. If this sounds like your situation, we strongly encourage you to seek professional help.

Thank You

We at Mometrix would like to extend our heartfelt thanks to you, our friend and patron, for allowing us to play a part in your journey. It is a privilege to serve people from all walks of life who are unified in their commitment to building the best future they can for themselves.

The preparation you devote to these important testing milestones may be the most valuable educational opportunity you have for making a real difference in your life. We encourage you to put your heart into it—that feeling of succeeding, overcoming, and yes, conquering will be well worth the hours you've invested.

We want to hear your story, your struggles and your successes, and if you see any opportunities for us to improve our materials so we can help others even more effectively in the future, please share that with us as well. **The team at Mometrix would be absolutely thrilled to hear from you!** So please, send us an email (support@mometrix.com) and let's stay in touch.

If you'd like some additional help, check out these other resources we offer for your exam:

http://mometrixflashcards.com/NCSF

Additional Bonus Material

Due to our efforts to try to keep this book to a manageable length, we've created a link that will give you access to all of your additional bonus material.

Please visit https://www.mometrix.com/bonus948/ncsf to access the information.